C O M P U T E R S

F O R

F A M I L Y   H I S T O R Y

AN INTRODUCTION

BY

D A V I D   H A W G O O D

MA, M.Inst.P, MBCS, FSG

HAWGOOD COMPUTING LIMITED

LONDON

Second edition, 1987

The photograph of Bramber, Sussex, on the front cover is from the postcard album of the author's grandmother Mrs Eva Hawgood. It was taken close to the Temperance Hotel next to the museum in Bramber. John and Louisa Hawgood ran the hotel in the 1890's after spending most of their lives in Brighton, where John Hawgood was noted as a swimming champion and secretary of the Brighton Swimming Club. Their daughters were still running the hotel when the photograph was taken. The caption reads:

> "Winner of tub race on highway from Bramber to Beeding during flood Feb 2 1904"

This book is dedicated

To **Mary Reidy**
who encouraged me to write my first book;

And to my wife **Barbara**
who has encouraged me to continue writing.

Copyright © David Hawgood 1987

Published by Hawgood Computing Limited,
26 Cloister Road, Acton, London W3 0DE.

First edition February 1985
Reprinted with minor corrections October 1985

Second edition November 1987

Typing and layout by David Hawgood.
Line illustrations (Chapter 2) by Brian Morse.
Photographs (Chapter 1) by David Hawgood.

Printed in Great Britain
by Parchment (Oxford) Ltd, 60 Hurst Street, Oxford.

British Library Cataloguing in Publication Data

Hawgood, David
Computers for family history: an introduction. ---2nd ed.
1. Genealogy-----Data Processing
I. Title
929'.1'02854   CS14

ISBN 0-948151-03-X

CONTENTS

PREFACE

My hobby is family history: my profession is computing. In 1981 I started using a home computer for family history, and encountered problems. Although I knew that a number of other people had used computers for genealogy, there did not seem to be any way of finding out how they had overcome the same problems. I wrote a letter to the Sussex Family Historian suggesting that a forum for interchange of experience was needed. The editor Frank Leeson suggested that I should start a magazine to cover this subject. He and Alexander Sandison, a pioneer in genealogical computing, persuaded the Society of Genealogists to publish the magazine. As a result I edited "Computers in Genealogy" for four years.

In this book I describe what I learnt, through my own use of computers and through the experience of others. The book is intended for the genealogist with no previous knowledge of computers. As I use each new technique, I describe the background to it in simple terms.

Most books which aim to provide an introduction to home computers start with an introduction to computer programming. This book does exactly the opposite. It tells you how to use a computer without having to learn how to program it. It says what can be done in family history using a computer at home.

I wish to thank all those whose contributions in magazine articles, conferences, meetings and discussion have contributed to the development of computing for family history. I started editing "Computers in Genealogy" to provide a forum for discussion, and I have learnt a great deal from other people's contributions. My aim in this book is to pass on this experience, without requiring readers to have previous knowledge of computing.

I also wish to thank Brian Morse, who drew the diagrams of disk, cassette, microdrive, microfilm and microfiche equipment. Particular thanks are due to Don Francis and Helen Cohen, who read a draft of the first edition and made helpful comments.

I wrote the first edition of this book in 1984. Since then computers have become cheaper. Many more people have computers at home as word processors. More genealogy packages are available. But the principles of using computers for family history have not changed. In revising the book in 1987, I have changed details but have preserved the original structure of the book. Many readers told me that they found the first edition helpful. I hope the second edition will continue to guide genealogists starting to use computers.

David Hawgood.
Acton, London W3.
November 1987.

INTRODUCTION

WHY ARE COMPUTERS USEFUL FOR FAMILY HISTORY?

1. The essence of family history is storing, processing and communicating information about people, their families, and events in their lives.

2. Computers are machines for storing, processing and communicating information.

3. Computers have become cheap enough to be used by the individual family historian at home.

4. To use a computer for family history it is not necessary to learn how to program a computer. Programs written by other people are available for use in family history.

COMPUTERS AND GENEALOGISTS

Genealogists are accustomed to handling organised information. The processes performed by computers in handling family history information are not novel to genealogists: computers store, select, search, sort, copy and print. But the way computers set about doing these things may be unfamiliar, and the way the genealogist tells the computer what to do is almost certain to be unfamiliar.

This book provides guidance on the unfamiliar aspects of computers. It also discusses types and organisation of information. Use of computers requires more detailed analysis of the information we use. I have found that putting information into a computer system has encouraged me to go back over my information, checking the sources, deciding just which piece of information led to a certain conclusion. I believe that the use of computers can make the genealogist more systematic and critical.

HOW MANY PEOPLE, HOW MUCH MONEY, HOW MUCH TIME?

The essence of genealogical computing is keeping and handling records about people. At one extreme, the Church of Jesus Christ of Latter Day Saints (the Mormon church) handles records of events in the lives of hundreds of millions of people, using computers costing millions of dollars. System development and entry of data for their International Genealogical Index has been in progress for twenty years already. At the other extreme, a computer costing a hundred pounds or so can handle a few hundred records in one personal family history. Using a program I had just bought and had not used before, I was able to create a one-name file for several hundred events within two days. Somewhere between, at one or two thousand pounds, we can handle a marriage index or census transcript with 50,000 records. This size of project is usually a co-operative effort taking between a few months and a couple of years. After a certain minimum needed to design a system, the time taken is almost entirely a matter of the time taken to enter data.

PEOPLE	MONEY
Hundreds	Hundreds
Tens of Thousands	A Thousand or so
Hundreds of millions	Millions

WHAT IS THE ADVANTAGE COMPARED WITH A CARD INDEX?

Compared with use of a card index, the primary advantage of a computer is that information can be arranged or selected in different ways. Index cards can easily be kept sorted in one order, for example alphabetical order of names. But I find I want information sorted in different ways. For example, using my computer I can sort records into family groups, or into date order, or by parish name. I can select which records to include in a list - only births in the 18th century, only events recorded in Sussex.

The second advantage is that it is easy to make additional copies of information, either in printed form or as magnetic recordings suitable to be read by computer. When I go to a record office, I take two lists of the records in my personal family history. One list is in date order within family groups, another in alphabetical order of names. Taking these lists reduces the risk that I will lose my records, and ensures that I always have a summary of all my family information when I am searching.

PLAN OF THIS BOOK

The first two chapters of this book describe computer equipment. The second chapter concentrates on the types of information genealogists need to store, and the ways computers can store it.

Chapter Three describes computer programs and software in outline. The next three chapters describe the pre-written programs that are useful in genealogy - database packages, word processing packages, and genealogy packages.

One question readers will be asking is "what computer should I buy?". This is the hardest to answer, as models and prices of computers in the shops change very fast. Appendix One describes some of the particular models of computer people use for genealogy, and some of the software available to run on them.

Appendix Two gives a list of books and magazines for further reading, details of relevant clubs and societies, and other useful addresses.

There is a full glossary. I found that this took on a life of its own when I was writing it, so you may find information in the glossary not covered in the rest of the book.

CHAPTER ONE

COMPUTERS

MAINFRAME COMPUTERS AND PERSONAL COMPUTERS

From 1962 to 1980 my work was with mainframe computers, which are large computers used for the work of many people within an organisation. These had magnetic tape drives the size of a wardrobe, printers and disk drives the size of a chest of drawers, and operating consoles the size of a desk. As for the central processor, that would have filled a pantechnicon by itself. The prices of these beasts were in the hundreds of thousands of pounds, to match their impressive bulk. The volume of information handled was equally impressive. One of the computers I worked on processed the weekly payroll for a quarter of a million miners. Another collected information about telephone bills from over a thousand keyboards connected to it from offices all over the country.

During this period the cost and size of the computers decreased with mass production and advances in technology. Improved techniques for making semiconductor circuits made it possible to put a processor on one chip of silicon. This is known a microprocessor, and a computer containing one is known as a micro-computer. This advance made it economic to produce a personal computer, small enough to fit on a desk top and cheap enough to be used by one person for his own work, rather than being a central facility for an organisation.

Micro-computers are now available which are not only small enough to fit on a desk, but small enough to carry around. The terms "transportable" or "luggable" are used for ones about the size of a sewing machine or suitcase. The term "portable" is used for ones about the size of an A4 writing pad which can reasonably be carried in a briefcase.

WHAT IS A COMPUTER?

A computer is an information processing machine which accepts input information, automatically processes it, and provides meaningful output in accordance with a set sequence of instructions held within it. Information can be stored and subsequently recalled. Figure 1 shows this:

Figure 1.

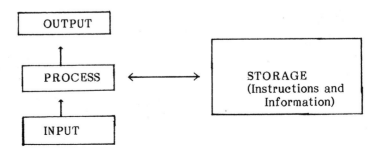

OUTPUT:
Display on
Television set

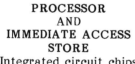

**PROCESSOR
AND
IMMEDIATE ACCESS
STORE**
Integrated circuit chips

STORAGE:
Cassette Recorder

INPUT: Keyboard

JARGON:
"HARDWARE","SOFTWARE", "INPUT", "OUTPUT", "DATA" AND "CHIPS"

In this chapter I describe some of the computer equipment sold for home use. In the next chapter I discuss the types of information stored by genealogists, and describe the computer equipment available to store it. Computer equipment is known in jargon as "hardware". Anything you can pick up or kick is hardware.

In Chapters 3 to 6 I discuss computer programs and the way they process information. Computer programs are known in jargon as "software". The term covers all programs, including those you write yourself, those supplied with the computer, and those available for sale.

"Input" means the transfer of information into the computer from outside, for example from a keyboard.

"Output" means the transfer of information from the computer to the outside in meaningful form, for example printing text on paper.

The terms "data" and "information" are often used as synonyms. If they are contrasted, data is the form held in a coded or structured way, for example recorded on a magnetic disk. Information is then the form meaningful to man as speech, pictures, printed text, etc.

A "chip" is any semi-conductor integrated circuit. The actual chip is a tiny piece of silicon about ¼" square. It may contain thousands of individual transistors formed in the semi-conducting silicon. It is housed in a casing of plastic about 1" long with electrical connections coming out to a row of pins either side. One integrated circuit may be a processor, or some storage, or the control circuits for other input, output, or storage devices. Storage in which information is recorded on moving media such as magnetic tapes or disks is called "backing store".

HOME COMPUTERS

Figure 2 expands the "input, process, storage, output" diagram to show the corresponding pieces of home computer equipment.

The cheapest type of home computer is sold as a keyboard unit, housing a processor and semi-conductor store. It has control circuits and connections allowing use of a domestic television set to display output, and use of a domestic cassette recorder as backing storage. Most of the computers being bought now for use in genealogy do not require these external connections. Instead they have a display screen and disk storage built in. Particular models of computer are described in Appendix One.

INPUT

On all home computers input can be made from a keyboard. The one shown in Figure 2 is on my Tandy Model 4 computer. It has a layout similar to a typewriter keyboard, with some extra keys for control - here we have ENTER, BREAK, CLEAR, and CTRL (short for "Control"). There is also an additional set of number keys, laid out like a calculator, and three "function keys" F1, F2, and F3. The functions of these can be defined within a program - as I type this F1 means "insert" and F2 means "delete". There are also arrow keys to move the cursor up, down, left, and right on the display screen. (The cursor is a special character displayed on the screen to show the current typing position).

If you are buying a computer and intend to input large amounts of data, for example a one name study or a transcription project, make sure the keyboard is one on which you can type comfortably.

PROCESSOR

Although the processor is the most important part of the computer, you are unlikely to be aware of it as a physical object. It is just one of the integrated circuit packages plugged onto a circuit board.

The term "central processor" includes both the processor and the semi-conductor storage. This expresses the very close relationship between them.

STORE

Figure 2 shows one type of magnetic recording device used as backing storage on home computers, a domestic casette recorder. The other main type used is a disk drive. These are described in the next chapter. The major difference is that access to information on tape is serial - you have to read down the tape from the start to find a piece of information. On a disk, access is random - the recording head can be moved over the surface of the disk to obtain any piece of information directly. Also, information transfer is faster on disks. But disks are considerably more expensive.

TYPES OF SEMI-CONDUCTOR STORE

In one section of semiconductor store, the read only memory (abbreviated as "ROM"), data is stored permanently. It is still available even after the computer has been turned off and on again. The user cannot change this data.

Another section of semiconductor store is termed the Random Access Memory (abbreviated as "RAM"). The user can change the data in it. Data in this is destroyed if the computer is turned off completely. Some computers, particularly small portable ones, have a form of random access memory in which the contents are retained with very small power consumption - the data is lost only if left without batteries.

The random access memory and read only memory together are the immediate access memory. The processor can obtain any piece of information in this at electronic speed - within microseconds (a microsecond is a millionth of a second). Individual storage locations are numbered, and the processor uses these numbers as addresses in storing and retrieving information.

A micro-computer described as having "64K" has 64 kilobytes of immediate access store. A kilobyte contains 1024 bytes, and is abbreviated as Kbyte or just K. A byte holds one character. Thus "64K" is 65,536 characters of information.

This brings me on to the difference between "8-bit" and "16-bit" computers. 8-bit computers can only use numbers up to 65,536 in addressing individual characters in the store. 16-bit computers can use numbers up into the millions, but are limited to 640 kilobytes if compatible with the IBM Personal Computer.

There are ways of using more than 64 kilobytes on an 8-bit micro. One is to switch between several areas or 'banks' of store, for example a ROM holding a word processor program, another ROM holding a spreadsheet program. Another way is to treat the extra store as if it was a disk, selecting an area of a few hundred characters from the 'memory drive' and moving it to be within the top 64K. All of this manipulation is done for you by the computer system.

OUTPUT

DISPLAY SCREENS

For display many home computers use a domestic television set as shown in Figure 2. The computer provides output from a TV aerial socket in the same range of frequencies as a broadcast television signal, and one channel of the TV set has to be tuned to the right frequency to detect it. Other computers use a "monitor" - this is like a television set but the computer provides a lower frequency "video" signal which controls the screen directly, rather than a transmission frequency signal. The display using a video signal on a monitor can be clearer than the display using a transmission frequency. You may encounter the term "RGB" - it is the name of the interface for a video signal including colour. A few computers have both transmission and video output sockets.

Some small portable computers have a flat display screen, like that in a calculator. So far the number of characters displayed on these has been rather limited, but they are becoming larger.

PRINTERS

You will almost certainly want a printer if you are using a computer to assist your family history research. You can probably choose a printer after deciding what computer and programs you will use. But if you particularly need a printer giving quality equivalent to that of an electric typewriter, make sure that one is available for the computer and programs you are choosing.

The possibility of printing large numbers of characters per line is very useful for family trees - but see Chapter 5 on word processing for alternatives.

Printers are becoming cheaper. Like all things in micro-computers, if in doubt buy a cheap one that satisfies your initial requirements.

TYPES OF PRINTER

1. DOT MATRIX PRINTERS

From about £100 these print at least 80 normal-size characters per line on ordinary paper 9" wide or more, at about 80 characters per second. The characters are formed by a row of tiny wires which press an inked ribbon onto the paper to form the letter shape from dots. A variety of styles and sizes can be produced, including compressed print allowing at least 130 characters per line. Even cheap dot matrix printers now have a 'near letter quality' (NLQ) mode in which the character shapes are improved by printing each line twice, the second pass filling in the spaces between the dots left by the first pass.

More expensive printers may allow wider paper, more choice of stationery, more choice of characters including lines and symbols. Use of more wires in the print head, and closer spacing of rows of dots, give clearer letter shapes.

As every dot on the paper can be controlled separately, this gives great flexibility to include different typefaces and larger headings. Dot matrix printers can also produce graphics - diagrams and pictures. The combination of text, headings and graphics has become known as "Desk Top Publishing".

2. DAISY WHEEL PRINTERS AND ELECTRIC TYPEWRITERS

All these printers have a variety of typefaces available on interchangeable golf-balls, thimbles, or daisy wheels (which hold their type elements on radial petal-like spokes, hence the name).

Daisy wheel printers, which started at £2000 a few years ago, are now available for £200 or less. All give good typewriter quality printing. The cheaper models print at about 12 characters per second, may have less than 90 different characters available, and have no sprockets for fan-fold paper.

If you want high quality printing make sure the facilities you want are available in the printer and can be controlled from the programs you will be using. This may sound obvious, but it is only too easy to find they are "not quite" compatible – if only that the key marked £ doesn't print as £. When I decided to buy a daisy wheel printer I spent quite a long time investigating printers and word processing software. In the end I bought both from Tandy, the makers of my computer, because I could control bold printing, underlining, justified proportional spaced printing, 15 character per inch printing, and accented letters, all from within the word processing software.

The text of this book is printed using a daisy wheel printer. Figure 3 shows examples of dot matrix printing, all from one Epson printer.

Figure 3. Examples of Dot Matrix Printing

NORMAL	**CONDENSED**	**ENHANCED**
JOHN EVELINE MARY THOMAS	JAMES CARVER 1792-1845 DRAPER WARMINSTER = (1824) SARAH ROGERS 1801-1871	**FAMILY TREE**

3. LASER PRINTERS

Laser printers use the principles of eloctrostatic photocopiers. A laser draws the required image, ink particles stick to the image and are pressed onto the paper. The definition of the image is better than that from a dot matrix printer. Laser printers are available from £1500. Bear in mind if considering one that the running costs are much higher.

FRICTION FEED, SPROCKET FEED, AND STATIONERY

When I first bought a computer to use at home, I thought I would mainly look at information on the screen of the computer, occasionally printing an extract from it. In the event I have printed long program listings, books, magazines, numerous lists of events and people in my family history, and family trees. I have also printed business letters, mailing labels, and duplicator stencils.

You may not end up with quite such a variety of printing, but will almost certainly produce both single sheets of text as letters, and quite long lists of people. There is a definite advantage in having a printer with sprocket feed, preferably variable width. I prefer to have friction feed as well.

Friction feed uses the same principle as an ordinary typewriter, a spring loaded roller, and can handle paper without sprocket holes - letter headings, envelopes, etc. It can also handle rolls or fan-fold paper, but these tend to wander sideways after a few pages. Sprocket feed pulls the paper through by holes spaced down the sides, so the paper stays straight.

Fan-fold paper has sprocket holes down the sides, and perforations so the sheets can be separated. "Tear down" paper also has perforations to allow the strip with the sprocket holes to be torn from the side, leaving a neat rectangular sheet. Fan-fold and tear-down paper are obtainable in different thicknesses - you can get the equivalent of good quality typing paper as well as thin listing paper. Small quantities are available from computer shops: a wider range is available from specialist mail order suppliers. Incidentally, printer ribbons are surprisingly expensive - typically £3 for an Epson dot matrix printer, but the range on different printers is from £1 to £15.

COMMUNICATIONS

A means of data transfer available on many home microcomputers is a connection to another computer. There is a standard connection for this known by the number of its specification, RS232. This is a serial interface, one on which the eight bits forming a character are sent down a wire one after the other. The opposite is a parallel interface: a character is sent as one unit, requiring eight wires. Printers are usually connected using a parallel interface: the standard developed by Centronics is often used.

Units known as modems and acoustic couplers convert the computer signals from an RS232 interface to a form which can be transmitted over the telephone network. As its name implies, the acoustic coupler does this by generating a sound from a speaker close to the telephone earpiece. The advantage of it is that it can be used with any telephone (of the round-earpiece pattern). The modem (short for MOdulator DEModulator) provides an electrical connection between the telephone line and the computer. It requires more effort to install, but can provide faster and more reliable transmission. If two computers are close to one another, in the same room for example, they can be connected using the RS232 interfaces without any modem or acoustic coupler; this is a convenient way of transferring data between otherwise incompatible computers.

There is a special data format called GEDCOM for communicating genealogical data: see the end of Chapter 6 for a description.

CHAPTER TWO

INFORMATION AND ITS STORAGE

This chapter first describes the types of information which family historians may wish to store, then describes the ways of storing the information. Later chapters describe ways of processing the various types of information.

TABLES, TEXT, AND FAMILY TREES

If we are to use an information processing machine, we have to consider the nature of information. Below I show three of the arrangements of information we use in genealogy. The first is a table: the information is in rows and columns. It is an extract from a census enumerator's book, which has a line for each person and columns for the various items of information to be filled in. A large proportion of the information we use is arranged in tables, or in lists which are simpler versions of the same arrangement.

TABLE:

1851 Census for 2 Temperance Place, St Pauls, Lincoln
(HO107/2105 folio 567/8)

Name & Surname	Rel.	Cond	Age M	Age F	Occupation	Where Born
William Lilburn	Head	Mar	35		Police Constable	Lincoln
Sarah Lilburn	Wife	Mar		32	Wife	York, Malton
Jane do	Dtr	Unm		13	Scholar	Lincoln
Geo do	Son	Unm	8		Scholar	do
(four more children are listed)						

Original headings of the above columns:
    Name and Surname of each person,
    Relation to head of family
    Condition,
    Age of   Males, Females (two separate columns)
    Rank, Profession or Occupation
    Where born

TEXT:

The second arrangement is text. What is shown is a piece of descriptive family history. The structure of information is that of the English language. The sub-divisions are paragraphs, sentences, and words.

> When my mother used to visit her grand-father in Lincoln, he told her about his own father William Lilburn, who was a police detective-inspector in Lincoln. His family particularly remembered that he went about his duties on a bicycle. I have a small police truncheon, marked with the arms of the City of Lincoln and with Queen Victoria's cypher, which must have belonged to William Lilburn.

FAMILY TREE STRUCTURE:

The third arrangement is a family tree. This is a diagrammatic representation of the structure of the family. The information is shown using some conventions which are familiar to all genealogists. The = (equals sign) shows a marriage, the names arranged across the page under a horizontal line are the children of that marriage.

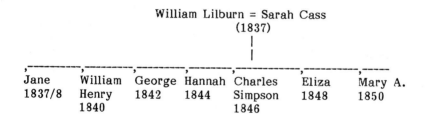

```
                    William Lilburn = Sarah Cass
                             (1837)
                               |
                               |
 ,---------,---------,---------,-------,------------,---------,----
 Jane      William   George    Hannah  Charles      Eliza     Mary A.
 1837/8    Henry     1842      1844    Simpson      1848      1850
           1840                        1846
```

There is information about my great-great grandfather William Lilburn in all these, presented in different ways. Computers have correspondingly different ways of holding and processing these types of information. These are listed in the table below, and explained in Chapters 4, 5 and 6.

Information	Processing package
Table	Database
Text	Word processor
Family structure	Genealogy package

FILES, RECORDS, FIELDS, AND CHARACTERS

We can use the example of a table of information to explain some of the terms used to describe information in computers.

A record is a collection of related items of information treated as a unit. In this table, each line is a record, containing the name, age , occupation etc of one person. Thus we have a record:

William Lilburn/ Head/ Mar/ 35/ /Police Constable/ Lincoln

A field is a piece of information, one item of data. If we take the record for William Lilburn, the information in each column is a separate field. There is a field for name, one for occupation, etc. The census book had one column to contain "name and surname", so in this case both are in one field. If we had a column headed "Forenames" and one headed "Surname", that would be two separate fields. Also the census enumerator's book had separate columns for "age of males" and "age of females". The latter field is of course empty in William Lilburn's record.

The information in a field is built up from individual characters: letters, digits, punctuation marks, etc.

It is not normally necessary to think about any unit smaller than a character. The computers we use are binary digital electronic computers. This means that they are built from circuits which have only two states, "on" or "off". Eight of these circuits are used to hold each character. For example if the second and eighth circuits are turned on, with the rest turned off, that is the code for a letter "A". One circuit holds one bit of information, short for "binary digit". Eight bits form a byte, short for "by eight", which normally holds one character. But there is no need to know about this to use a computer.

A file is an organised collection of related records. Thus the complete table is a file, with a record for each person. Often each record in a file contains a similar set of fields (for example name, age, occupation etc for each person). But there can be records in a file with additional or different fields. Fields can be of fixed or variable length, records can have fixed or variable numbers of fields.

Figure 1: File, Record, Field, Character

		Field	Field	Field	Field	Field
	(Record:	William Lilburn	Head	Mar	35	
File	(Record:	Sarah Lilburn	Wife	Mar		32
	(Record:	Jane do	Dtr	Unm		13
	(Record:	Geo do	Son	Unm	8	

```
|U |n |m |  |8 |  |  |
 ↑   ↑   ↑   ↑  ↑    ↑    ↑
--------Characters ---
```

HOW INFORMATION IS STORED: CASSETTE TAPES AND FLOPPY DISKS
SEQUENTIAL AND DIRECT ACCESS

"Backing Storage" is storage in which information is recorded on some medium which is physically moved past a reading head to transfer the information to the processor. It takes from a few thousandths of a second up to a few minutes to obtain information, depending on the device used.

Most home computers use either cassette tape or floppy disk for storage. Cassette tape is cheaper, but slower, and limited in facilities. Cassette computers are being sold mainly for games use, with very limited word processing and database software available. As computers with disks have become cheaper, I would no longer consider buying a computer with cassette storage for genealogical use. Some Sinclair computers use a compromise, the Microdrive, in which a loop of tape moves round very fast, giving the facilities of a floppy disk at lower equipment cost.

CASSETTE STORAGE

The cassette recorders used for microcomputers are the same as those used in home audio equipment and dictating machines. On a cassette, information is recorded as one track along the tape. It has to be retrieved by playing the tape from the start until the particular information is found. This is termed "Sequential Access".

Almost all microcomputers use cassettes by moving the whole of a file into immediate access store. The file might typically be up to 16000 characters. If information is changed, the whole new file has to be stored on a cassette. It is not possible to move the tape back and change an individual record.

Figure 2.
Cassette

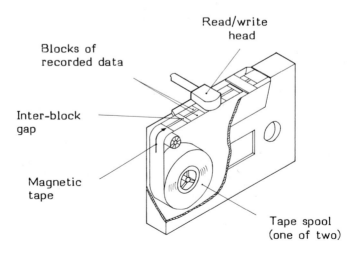

Read/write head

Blocks of recorded data

Inter-block gap

Magnetic tape

Tape spool (one of two)

FLOPPY DISK

Information is recorded on a floppy disk as concentric tracks - usually 40 or 80. The tracks are divided into sectors, typically holding 256 characters each. It is possible to read any individual sector, without reading all those before it in the file. This is called direct access, or random access.

The recording head moves in or out to a track. The disk rotates under the head. As the required sector moves under the head, the information in it is copied into the immediate access store. Any individual sector can be read into immediate access store, changed, and written back to its original position.

Figure 3. Floppy Disk.

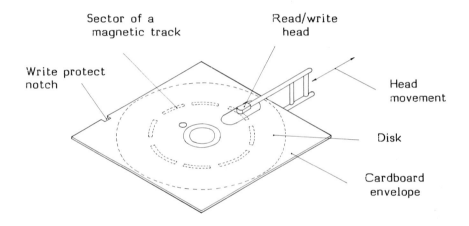

A variant of the floppy disk becoming available on some computers is the "hard case" disk. These have a higher recording density, so the disk can be smaller - between 3" and 4" diameter, compared with the 5¼" diameter of most floppy disks.

A "hard disk" is a disk with the recording surface coated on a rigid metal disk. Until recently, mainframe computers used hard disks, and microcomputers used floppy disks. But hard disks are becoming cheaper, and are now available for microcomputers. They give faster access - tens instead of hundreds of milliseconds. More important, they have a much greater capacity - typically ten million characters, compared with floppy disk capacities varying from 60,000 to a million characters.

MICRODRIVE

Figure 4 is a diagram of a Sinclair Microdrive. The microdrive cartridge contains a continuous loop of tape about 16 feet long, which is held on one spool. The tape feeds from the centre of the spool, past the recording head, and back to the outside of the spool. The capacity of a microdrive is about 100,000 bytes. There are other tape loop devices on the market as well, but the Sinclair Microdrive is the best known.

Figure 4.
Microdrive

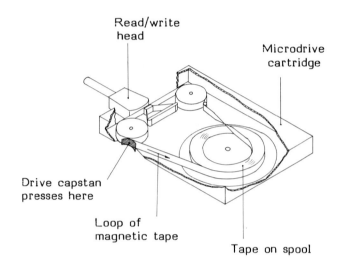

Read/write head

Microdrive cartridge

Drive capstan presses here

Loop of magnetic tape

Tape on spool

When I was buying my first microcomputer the extra facilities available made me decide to buy a system with disks. However other people have done a great deal of excellent family history work with cassette systems.

There can be several files on a cassette, or on a floppy disk. To allow quick access, the disk has a directory containing the names of the files on it and the numbers of the tracks and sectors they occupy. On a cassette tape, the name of the file is recorded on the tape just before the data for that file. It is necessary for the computer to read down the tape until the correct file name is found, then read the data from that file into immediate access store.

One aspect to investigate when deciding what system to buy is the cost of the media - the tape cassettes, floppy disks, microdrive cartridges, etc. Cassettes are available from 50 pence, floppy disks from £1.50, microdrive cartridges are £2. Looking around my shelves, I have nearly 200 floppy disks - a considerable investment.

SEQUENTIAL AND DIRECT ACCESS

It may help to think of a cassette tape as being like a microfilm, where you have to look along the film from the start to find the frame you want: access is sequential, frame after frame. By this analogy, a disk is like a microfiche, on which a selected frame can be moved under the lens if its row and column number are known: access is direct. The figure shows microfilm and microfiche, to compare with cassette tape and disk.

Figure 5 . Microfilm and Microfiche

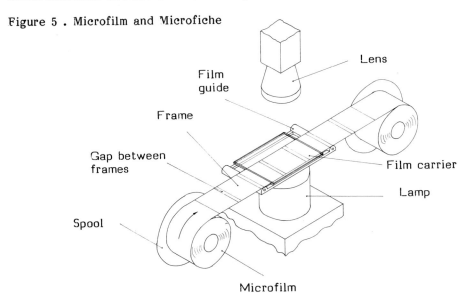

Microfilm

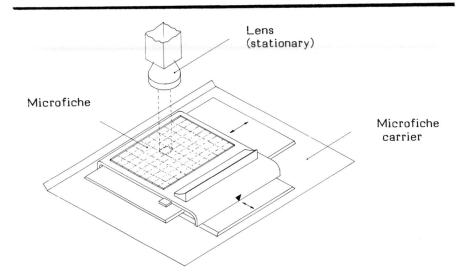

INFORMATION STORAGE – SPACE NEEDED AND SPACE AVAILABLE

HOW MUCH SPACE IS NEEDED?

A PAGE OF TEXT: 3000 CHARACTERS

A single spaced page of text is typically 60 lines of 60 characters, a total of 3600 characters. Allowing for headings, part lines and blank lines at the end of paragraphs gives an average of 3000 characters.

AN EVENT: 80 CHARACTERS

A baptism for example needs fields for names of the person, father, and mother, a date, and a place. On average this totals 80 characters.

A PERSON'S BIRTH, MARRIAGE, AND DEATH: 200 CHARACTERS

This needs four names (person, father, mother, spouse), with the date, place and source reference for three events. On average this totals 200 characters.

Some people have several spouses. Names, places and source references vary greatly in length. Space may be reduced by using reference numbers and abbreviations. Thus there can be substantial differences in the space needed. But these figures are a useful rule of thumb.

HOW MUCH SPACE IS AVAILABLE?

A CASSETTE FILE: 80 PEOPLE OR 200 EVENTS OR 5 PAGES OF TEXT

Most microcomputer systems handle cassette files by loading the complete file into immediate access store, manipulating the information there, then copying the changed file onto a cassette. A typical cassette file would allow 16,000 characters of data on a "32K" microcomputer. The figure available depends on the program in use, and the amount of random access memory available in the micro-computer.

A FLOPPY DISK: 320 PEOPLE OR 800 EVENTS OR 20 PAGES OF TEXT

This is for a single sided single density floppy disk which has about 64,000 characters left for data after formatting. Floppy disks are available holding up to a million characters.

A HARD DISK: 48,000 PEOPLE OR 120,000 EVENTS OR 3000 PAGES

A typical hard disk available for a micro-computer holds about ten million characters.

CHAPTER THREE

PROGRAMMING AND SOFTWARE

WHAT IS SOFTWARE

I have said that a computer processes information "in accordance with a set sequence of instructions held within it".

That sequence of instructions is the computer program.

In computer jargon, programs are "software". This term means all the programs which run on a computer for any reason. It includes programs written by the user, and pre-written programs available from the computer manufacturer and others. It includes application programs, which process data to provide information for the computer user. It also includes the "operating system": a variety of programs which are used in managing the data within the computer and providing the user with a convenient way of controlling the computer.

I described in Chapter 2 various ways in which information is organised, and listed the pre-written programs which can process them: database packages for lists and tables, word processing packages for text, genealogy packages for family linked structures. The next three chapters describe these packages. This chapter provides an introduction to computer programs.

The facilities available to make it easy to write programs, and the availability of pre-written programs, had a major influence on which particular computer I bought. As I used my computer, and learnt how other people were using their computers for genealogy, I wrote less programs myself and used pre-written programs more.

I have been surprised to discover what a large proportion of the requirements for family history computing can be satisfied by database packages. In the United Kingdom, most of the people using microcomputers for family history are using database packages. In the United States there have been substantial sales of genealogy packages. I will describe both these approaches. I would certainly recommend anyone commencing on family history computing to try a database package or genealogy package before embarking on writing any programs.

My other preliminary comment is that almost everyone I know who has a computer at home uses it extensively as a word processor. Most of this use is for typing and editing straightforward text. Word processors are also used for storing the descriptive matter of family history. Surprisingly, they provide a good way of producing family trees.

Before describing the various types of package, I will introduce some of the concepts of computer programs.

WHAT IS A COMPUTER PROGRAM

To look at the type of sequence of instructions which might form a computer program, consider the steps you follow in searching register indexes. This is an activity, familiar to most genealogists, which requires just the type of methodical and repetitive procedure which is handled well by computers. I am assuming that for each year there is one book, containing an index to all entries for that year, in alphabetical order of surname. I show the procedure in two ways. The first, shown in Figure 1, is a sequence of statements in English. These are fairly close to the way the statements would be expressed in a computer language like BASIC. The statements in Figure 1 are less formalised than a computer language, and some of the statements are redundant, but in essence this is the type of sequence which forms a computer program. Figure 2 is another way of showing the procedure, a diagrammatic representation called a flow-chart. This is a convenient and standardised way of showing a procedure. Rectangular boxes are operations, the flowlines are followed from one operation to the next, from top to bottom and left to right unless arrows indicate otherwise. Diamond shape boxes show decisions, points where different paths can be followed: the various alternative flow-lines leave the corners of the diamond.

FIGURE 1   PROGRAM IN ENGLISH STATEMENTS

    Input the first year, final year, and search-name.
    Set year equal to first year.

A   Get book for year.
        Open book at first page.
        Set count equal to zero.

B   If you have reached the end of the book, go forward to C.
        If not, read next name:
                If name is before search-name, go back to B;
                If name is after search-name, go forward to C;

                If name is the same as search-name:
                        Print name, forename, district and reference,
                        Add 1 to count,
                        Go back to B.

C   Print year, print count, print the word "entries".
        Advance paper one line without printing.
        If year is less than final year, then add 1 to year and go to A.
        If year equals or is after final year, then stop.

Figure 2
FLOWCHART

Programs & Software 21

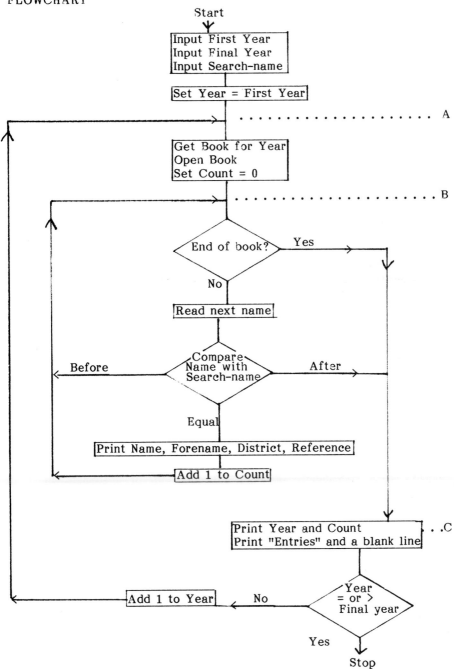

We decide what period to search and for what name, take down a book from the shelf and open it on the bench, search for the particular name, and write down the details if that name appears. We look for more entries for the same name in that book, then go on to the next book.

This procedure contains various elements very common in computer programs:

Decision: Is it the right name? Is it the final year?
Repetition: after reading a name, and deciding if it is the one of interest, you read the next name and repeat the process. When you have finished with one book, you repeat the procedure on the next book. This repetition is known as a loop.
Input: years and name to search
Retrieving stored information
Output - we write down the entries found, the year, and a count of entries for the year
End conditions: we have to decide what to do if we reach the end of the book before reaching the name of interest - if the name is Zwemmer for example. The test for this condition appears as a decision.
Error conditions: does the procedure work if the "final year" is before the "first year"?

It may have occurred to you that looking at every name in the book until you find the one of interest is rather wasteful of effort. There are various more efficient strategies. The first improvement would be to look at the name at the bottom of the page first, then decide whether to read through that page. More improvement would come from opening the book at about the right place, and turning forward or back as necessary.

These various strategies are different algorithms for searching the book for a particular name. An algorithm is a formal statement of a procedure for solving a problem - it must be one that leads to a solution in a finite number of steps. An algorithm can be communicated in various ways, for example as a flowchart, mathematical equation, or statement in plain language.

To turn it into a computer program, the procedure has to be broken down into small steps and expressed in a language the computer can understand. For example in the language BASIC which is available on most microcomputers, one statement of the procedure could be:

IF NAME = SEARCHNAME THEN PRINT NAME, FORENAMES, DISTRICT, REFERENCE

The computer interprets this statement and converts it into even smaller steps expressed in terms of the individual operations available on the particular processor.

The program has to allow for every eventuality. In the example given, there would have to be instructions to follow if the next book in sequence was missing, and instructions to follow if there is no room to open the book on the bench (squeeze in and start nudging your neighbours until you have enough room!).

PROGRAMMING LANGUAGES

The computer program has to contain precise instructions on the processing to be performed at each step, where to get the information to be processed, and where to put the result.

"High level computer languages" provide a way of giving those instructions in terms appropriate to the type of problem.

FORTRAN, short for "Formula Translation, was developed for practical use by scientists. A = B + C is an example of a simple Fortran statement.

BASIC (Beginners' All-purpose Symbolic Instruction Code) was derived from Fortran as an interactive language, intended to allow the user to conduct a conversation with the computer. IF A = 2 PRINT "CORRECT" is an example.

COBOL (Common Business-Oriented Language) was developed as a standard language for business data processing, aiming to allow the same statements to be used on different manufacturers' machines. The statements are intended to resemble English, for example **ADD OVERTIME TO BASIC-PAY GIVING GROSS-PAY.**

ALGOL (Algorithmic language) is intended as a mathematical notation as well as a computer programming language. There are a number of other languages derived from it, for example **PASCAL** which is currently the most fashionable language to teach computer science students. It is named after the famous French mathematician.

All high level computer languages have some features in common:

1. There is a precise set of rules for the syntax of statements. The order of expressions within a statement and the precise punctuation are all laid down. For example if a comma is missed the results may be quite different from those intended.

2. There is a way of defining the decisions to be taken, and changing the order in which statements are obeyed as a result of calculations and comparisons. A number of statements may be grouped together as a "routine" or "procedure", which may be given a name. The next routine to be obeyed may be given by its name, or by the number of the line in the program at which it starts.

3. There is a way of defining the locations and types of data to be manipulated. For example a particular field in store may contain a number, or it may contain a string of letters. For the convenience of the programmer, the field can be given a name (e.g. BIRTHDATE) rather than a numbered address.

A "low level" computer language is written in statements which are much closer in structure to the individual operations performed by the electronic circuits of the computer. A program in "machine code" is held in the form of numbered operations and addresses which can be acted on directly by the computer.

HOW YOU CAN USE A COMPUTER FOR FAMILY HISTORY - WITHOUT WRITING PROGRAMS

For those interested in writing their own programs, there are a number of articles in "Computers in Genealogy" and the American journal "Genealogical Computing" with program listings and descriptions of techniques.

But it is not necessary to write programs to use a computer for family history. It is helpful to understand that the computer works down a sequence of instructions. Some instructions cause a jump backwards or forwards to a different place in the sequence, deciding what to do on the basis of the results of previous operations. It is also helpful to understand that a computer program has to cater not only for correct data, but for errors. A good program will detect errors and allow them to be corrected - but this makes the program bigger and more complicated.

There are pre-written package programs which will allow you to do most of the processing you need. Furthermore, they are often efficiently written, so that they are likely to run faster than a program you write yourself for the purpose. Computer programming is a fascinating exercise. There is considerable satisfaction in seeing results from a program you have written yourself. But if your primary aim is sorting out your family history records, and sending the results of your research to other members of the family, pre-written packages are available to help you. They are described in the next three chapters. Before going on to these I will add some information on the important areas of security, data protection, and privacy.

SECURITY

Computer datafiles represent substantial effort in preparation. Purchased computer programs represent a considerable investment. Making an extra copy of a computer file is easier than making a copy of a document on paper. It is also very much easier to destroy the information on a computer file. It becomes essential to be methodical in keeping security copies of your computer files, known also as back-up copies.

WHAT ARE WE GUARDING AGAINST

1. Our Own Mistakes
By far the most likely way to destroy information is to make a mistake. Not only beginners make mistakes, experienced computer operators make them. You should aim to keep security copies so that you can recover

quickly when you make a mistake.

The minimum immediate protection is to keep a copy of a file with a different name, on the same disk or tape. I take a copy every half hour or so when creating or amending a file. There should also be a copy on a different disk or cassette, kept in the cupboard. Good practice is to make a fresh copy of any file you have changed at the end of every day. (Use the grandfather - father - son principle described below.) In a commercial installation, the "cupboard" should be a fire-proof safe (available from the supplies firms listed in Appendix 2.)

It is fatally easy to make the same mistake twice, so observe this GOLDEN RULE: If you accidentally erase or corrupt the working copy of a file, make another security copy from the back-up version, with a name not used previously, before putting the back-up into use.

2. Mistakes and Limitations in Computer Programs
It is extremely hard to test every conceivable use of a computer program. Mistakes are found in programs which have been in every-day use for years. Computer programs sometimes work correctly until the space available for data is completely filled, or some variable reaches its maximum value - then freeze up completely.

As protection, use the "grand-father, father, son" principle. The first file to be created becomes the son. In the next run this is read in as father, and the modified file which is written is the son. In the third run, the father becomes the grandfather, the son becomes the father, and a new son is created. On the fourth and subsequent runs the son is read: the file written in this run becomes the son, the son becomes the father, the father becomes the grandfather, and the grandfather is available for re-use.

3. Computer mal-function, or power failure
The computer may stop working, losing data in memory. A disk or tape may be magnetically or physically damaged.

Protection: save your data regularly, and keep a copy in the cupboard. If you buy a computer program, make two copies. Put the original and one copy away, use the second copy for work. (Note: some programs are protected against multiple copying, but there should be a way of making at least one copy.)

4. Fire, Flood, Theft
(Who would steal a computer disk? A child "needing" one to make a copy of the latest space invader game, that's who!)

Protection: Keep a copy away from your house.

Personally I have lost small amounts of data through my own mistakes, through computer malfunctions, and through oddities in purchased computer programs. I have usually recovered in five to ten minutes, using my security copies. On one occasion the directory on a disk with my only copies of some word processor files became corrupt, and it took me a few very anxious hours to re-build the directory. On another occasion a computer was stolen from me, and the disks near it were taken as well. I have been more careful about keeping security copies since then. It is so easy to make extra copies of files, and takes so much time to input the data again, that it is well worth keeping a copy away from home.

5. Computer Obsolescence
In due course you will outgrow your computer, or it will break and not be worth mending.

Protection: in some cases you will be able to transfer your old files directly to the new computer. If your software has an option to generate ASCII files, use it occasionally to keep security copies of your most important files. An ASCII file is one in which the control codes peculiar to the program generating the file have been stripped out. This makes it easier to read the file into a different program later on. ("ASCII" is short for American Standard Code for Information Interchange - it is the character code used on most micro-computers.) Some genealogy packages now have a utility to transfer files into a special data transfer format called "GEDCOM", a standard initiated by the Mormon Church. This also provides transfer of files between different machines and packages.

In practice I find that the information is so much better organised after I have entered it into a computer system, edited, added, and corrected, that I enter it again from a listing on paper.

PRIVACY AND DATA PROTECTION

If you keep in your computer information about living persons you will have to comply with the provisions of the Data Protection Act, and may have to register. (The address of the Data Protection Registrar is given in Appendix 2)

The reasons why computer records need more stringent provisions concerning privacy than paper records are just those reasons which make computers useful for genealogy: it is possible to accumulate and copy files about large numbers of persons, and search those files in ways not envisaged when the data was entered.

The Data Protection Act gives exemption from registration where data is kept for domestic or recreational purposes, or solely for preparing documents. A Society of Genealogists leaflet clarifies the exemptions: see Appendix 2. Amateur family historians are usually exempt.

What I have decided for my own computing at present is that the only living persons in my genealogy computer files are members of my own family, and my wife's family.

CHAPTER FOUR

DATA HANDLING AND DATABASE PACKAGES

The database packages available on home computers handle information which can be arranged as lists or tables. One example is part of a one name study, a list of deaths from the General Registry Office index:

Year	Quarter	Surname	Forenames	Age	Registration District	Ref
1894	Mar	Hawgood	Helen V	32	Christchurch	2b 481
1894	Jun	Hawgood	Ellen Elizabeth	3	Fulham	1a 205
1894	Sep	Hawgood	-			
1894	Dec	Hawgood	-			
1895	Mar	Hawgood	Charles Augustus	0	Greenwich	1d 841

Database packages first give facilities to define the fields to be used - in effect the column headings in a table. The other processes available are just those most useful to genealogical record keeping:

    Enter data
    Edit data
    Store
    Search
    Select
    Sort
    Display
    Print

The precise facilities vary, but the basis is always the same. Database packages available on mainframe computers have much more complex facilities; the people familiar with these do not even regard the packages available on home computers as being worthy of the name "database", and prefer to call them "data handling packages". For the purposes of this book, I will call them all databases.

USING A DATABASE FOR EVENTS AND INDEXES

Recently I extracted the first few years of births, marriages, and deaths for "Excell" and similar surnames from the indexes at the General Registry Office. An extract is shown in the first table overleaf. I noticed that similar names and places occurred in the births and deaths - probably infant deaths. Even in the first quarter there is an example, with the birth of "Male Exell" and death of "Infant Male Exall" being registered in Dursley. Might they be the same? To look at this I entered the information into my database system and sorted the list in order of Christian name, and then date. The result is shown in the second table overleaf.

Births, Marriages, and Deaths for Excell and similar names: Sept 1837

Year	Quarter	Event	Surname	Christian names	Registration District
1837	Sep	D	Exall	Sarah	London
1837	Sep	D	Exall	Sarah Anne	Marylebone
1837	Sep	D	Excell	John	Reading
1837	Sep	D	Exell	Male Infant	Dursley
1837	Sep	B	Exall	Clara Susannah	Lambeth
1837	Sep	B	Excell	John	Hastings
1837	Sep	B	Excell	Male	Cheltenham
1837	Sep	B	Exell	Male	Hackney
1837	Sep	B	Exall	Male	Dursley
1837	Sep	M	Excell	John	Maidstone

Table of entries in the first year of registration, sorted into Christian Name and date order:

Yr & Quarter	Event	Surname	Christian names	Registration District
1837Q4	B	Excell	Alfred	Chipping Sodbury
1838Q2	B	Exell	Ann	Dursley
1837Q4	B	Excell	August Rogers	Warminster
1838Q3	D	Excell	Augustus Roger	Warminster
1837Q4	B	Excell	Avis	Maidstone
1838Q2	B	Exall	Charles Edward	Wokingham
1837Q3	B	Exall	Clara Susannah	Lambeth
1837Q4	M	Exall	Edward	Wokingham
1837Q4	B	Exel	Elizabeth	Henley
1837Q4	B	Excell	Female	Lewes
1837Q3	B	Excell	John	Hastings
1837Q3	D	Excell	John	Reading
1837Q3	M	Excell	John	Maidstone
1838Q2	B	Exell	John	Camberwell
1837Q4	D	Exell	Joseph	Bethnal Green
1837Q3	B	Excell	Male	Cheltenham
1837Q3	B	Exell	Male	Hackney
1837Q3	B	Exall	Male	Dursley
1837Q3	D	Exell	Male Infant	Dursley
1838Q2	B	Excell	Mary Wallar Coveill	Maidstone
1838Q2	D	Excell	Mary Wallar Coveill	Maidstone
1837Q4	B	Exall	Robert John	Chelsea
1838Q2	B	Exell	Rosanna	Kingsclere
1837Q3	D	Exall	Sarah	London
1837Q3	D	Exall	Sarah Anne	Marylebone
1837Q4	D	Excell	Thomas Walker Covell	Maidstone
1837Q4	D	Exell	William	St Giles Camberwell

Note that I entered the quarters as Q1, Q2, Q3, Q4. This is done to make the entries sort in chronological order. Otherwise the quarters would appear in alphabetical order of names of months, Dec Jun Mar Sep.

Some events are obviously linked. Poor little Mary Waller Coveill Excell had a name longer than her life - her birth and death were registered in the same quarter. The index shows "August Rogers Excell" born Warminster, "Augustus Roger Excell" died in Warminster the next year - surely that must be the same child. The small differences in the name may be an error at the time of registration, or a subsequent transcription error. In fact he was Augustus Rogers Excell, and came from my wife's branch of the Excell family.

So far the results are much the same as could be obtained from a card index. But having entered the information in my database, I was able to manipulate it in other ways. I sorted it by Registration District: in Wokingham this put together the marriage of Edward Exall and the birth of Charles Edward Exall. In Maidstone, Thomas Walker Covell Excell appears near Mary Waller Coveill Excell, which made me wonder even more about the accuracy of transcription. Of course I would have to obtain certificates, parish register entries, and other information to establish linkages between these people but this manipulation starts to indicate avenues worth exploring. Quite apart from these clues about possible linkages, the numbers appearing in each registration district give a picture of the distribution of the surname. The name Excell is supposed to derive from the village of Exhall in Warwickshire - it is odd that there are no registrations from that county in the list!

I can describe other facilities available in database software by reference to the same list.

I can edit the information: for example if I rechecked the index and found the transcription error was mine, I could change Thomas Walker Covell Excell to Thomas Waller Covell Excell, which is the way he appears on the death certificate I have.

I can add extra entries - for example I could add in the Axcell surname entries.

I can search for entries with specific contents. For example I can search for all entries in Dursley after the first quarter of 1838, or search for all entries containing the name "Edward". This would find "Edward" and "Charles Edward". Similarly a search for entries containing the letters "Ann" would find "Ann Exell" and "Sarah Anne Exall".

The database software I have used most on both Tandy Model 1 and Model 4 computers is "Datawriter", which is no longer available. I describe some of the ways I have used it in the next section, and have also described them in an article (Ref 1).

SOME DATABASE USERS

Probably the simplest database I have seen used for genealogy is the Microl database which Don Francis (Ref 2) has used on a Sinclair Spectrum. He used it for extracts for the single surname Bushby from parish registers. His typical entry is

727/04/14 Jhn s Wm & Amy x

which represents: 1727, April 14th,   John (Bushby) son of William and Amy christened.

In this database each record is one continuous line of 31 characters. This makes it very compact, with 1000 records on cassette in a 48K Spectrum. Records can be sorted by date, and searches can be made for records containing several specific pieces of information. For example, the file could be searched for records containing both "Wm" and "Amy"; this would find any siblings of the John Bushby in the record above. The database file is divided up into documents, each having as title the name of a parish.

*****

Keith Salkeld (Ref 3) has used the cassette version of a database called Quest on a BBC micro. This was for a one name study on his wife's surname Medlam. The application is similar to my own use of the Excell birth, marriage and death information described above - sorting, searching and printing to present the information in different ways and test hypotheses. The fields he uses are:

Parish   Chapman county code then place name, with type of place if not a parish (e.g. REG DIST for Registration District)
Name   Forenames and Surname
Event   e.g. BIRTH, BAP, RESID, MARR, DEATH
Date   Year/month/day numbers with slashes between. Unknown numbers are given as zero - e.g. 1839/06/00 for a June quarter registration.
Relation   Contains the names and relationships of other people mentioned in the event.
Notes   Shows whether a certificate has been obtained, and other information like age at death or occupation of father.

A typical entry is:
PARISH   SOM; BRISTOL ST AUGUSTINE
NAME   ROBERT JAMES MEDLAM
EVENT   BIRTH
DATE   1844/09/01
RELATION   F;ROBERT M;MARY ANN WILLIAMS
NOTES   CERT;F=PORTER

*****

Doreen Wilcocks (Ref 4) has used Masterfile with disks on a BBC micro for a project for the North Middlesex Family History Society. This is an index of about 5000 burials and memorial inscriptions in one cemetery. The fields and their lengths were:

Name   Surname then forenames, 25 characters (a few names had to be abbreviated)
Date   7 characters: year (without millenium), month and day in figures
Age   5 characters
Plot   10 characters (the number of the burial plot in the cemetery)
Parish All "CCB" for "Christ Church Barnet" in this cemetery. This field is present in the hope that the file can be amalgamated later with similar files from other places.
From   10 chars. Place of residence, if given.

An example is:

Name	Date	Age	Plot	Parish	From
Welch Elizabeth	9301004	69	A36	CCB	Hadley

Meaning: "on 4th October 1930 Elizabeth Welch, age 69, from Hadley, was buried in plot A36 of the cemetery in the parish of Christ Church, Barnet".

The 5000 records took 5 disks, split up alphabetically by surname into 20 files.

*****

David Barnard (Ref 5,6,7) has used a rather different database, called "GG-3". He has written it himself specifically for genealogical applications, and is selling a successor "GG-5" for use on the BBC micro with disks. He has organised the database so that different records can contain different types of information - for example if "Age", "Occupation", "Name of Spouse", "Name of Parents" etc are present in some burial records but not in others, only the ones for which information is available take up space. One specific example of use he describes is indexing 366 entries in a Militia list for Hitchin.

*****

I have a one name study for the Sapp family in Sussex. This uses Datawriter on my Tandy (Ref 1). I had two specific aims in this study. One was to compare the information I had obtained from different sources. The other was to find a way of listing together all records with references to a particular forename - e.g. Richard as son in a baptism, father in a baptism, husband in a marriage, executor to a will, tenant of a piece of land mentioned in a deed, etc. I used abbreviated forenames, as I wanted similar forenames to appear as the same (e.g Ann and Anne).

The fields I used were:

Forename, 1st person	Abbreviated, e.g Jn, Ric, Eliz, An, Thos
Surname, 1st person	In full
Relationship, 1st person	Abbreviated: s = son, d = daughter, w = wife, h = husband, m = mother, f = father, etc
Forename, 2nd person	)
Surname, 2nd person	) All as for
Relationship, 2nd person	) first person
Forename, 3rd person	)
Surname, 3rd person	)
Relationship, 3rd person	)
Event	One letter abbreviation, c for christened, m for married, etc
Date	9 characters: e.g. 1672-0818 for 18th Aug 1672
Place	Chapman County Code, then place name in full, e.g. SSX Walberton.
Record Type	abbreviated, e.g. pr for parish register
Record Reference	Repository, call number, and transcriber in full
Notes	e.g. "Can't read forename"
Linked event	10 characters; date of an earlier event for one of the people (the extra character allows for a question mark where the linkage is uncertain).

As I worked with this database, probable linkages became apparent. I added the "linked event" field to show these. I kept the definition loose. If possible a marriage is linked to the baptism of the Sapp partner in the marriage, a burial is linked to a baptism of the person buried, a baptism is linked to the marriage of the parents.

When I started this exercise, most of the records were ones I had tried to sort manually into families. As I added more events, for example from the International Genealogical Index, I found it convenient to sort the records by date of event within father's or husband's forename. In general, this sorts families together. For example:

Date	Event	-first----- person	-second--- person	-third---- person	Place
1782-0702	m	Mary w	Edmund h		SSX Petworth
1782-1117	c	David s	Edmund f	Mary m	SSX Petworth
1783-1201	c	Edmund s	Edmund f	Mary m	SSX Kirdford
1785-0624	c	Martha d	Edmund f	Mary m	SSX Kirdford
1785-0624	c	Mathew s	Edmund f	Mary m	SSX Kirdford
etc -					

There is a total of twelve children, some baptised in Petworth and some in Kirdford, who appear likely to belong to this one family.

USING A DATABASE FOR PERSONAL FAMILY HISTORY –
WITH LINKS, NUMBERS AND CROSS REFERENCES

Most simple database packages on home computers are not specifically designed to provide linkages between records. To show marriage and parentage links, the user has to build a structure into the records. Doing this can become fairly complicated. The newcomer to computing may be well advised to experiment with a file of individual unlinked events, as described above, before deciding what linkage is required.

I have found that most of the benefits of using a database come from being able to sort people by name, birthdate, birthplace, etc. This is also the simplest to carry out. I find the best way of showing family structure is by preparing a family tree, using a word processor. This is described in the next chapter. (There is a note at the end of this chapter about the preparation of family trees using data held in a database.)

Although it is complicated, it is possible to design the records and reference numbers to show marriage and parentage links. I find this worthwhile, and will describe two approaches to doing it. The fields in records with links to parents, spouse and children have to be different from those which are lists of events. It becomes necessary to allocate reference numbers to the people. Before describing the record structure, I will describe some numbering systems used in genealogy.

NUMBERING SYSTEMS

The simplest system is one in which every person is allocated a reference number arbitrarily. Several of the genealogy packages use arbitrary numbers – the first person entered gets the lowest number, whether you start entry from the earliest ancestor or the newest baby.

There are also several systematic numbering systems. The first is used for direct ancestors of one person:

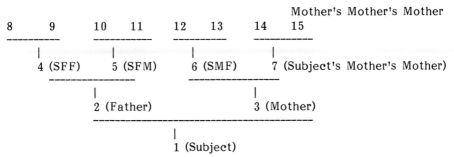

This is a standard numbering system which is used a great deal in the United States. The numbers can be derived from the relationships simply: an individuals number is doubled to give the number of the father; one more is added to give the number of the mother. This system can be extended for any number of generations. Great-great-grandparents are 16 to 31, g-g-g-grandparents are 32 to 63, etc.

A variant of this is to number the lines of descent – for example the eight great-grandparents lines are numbered from line 1 (father's father's father and ancestors) to 8 (mother's mother's mother and ancestors).

An alternative numbering system works on the descendents from one person. In my example this progenitor is person "A":

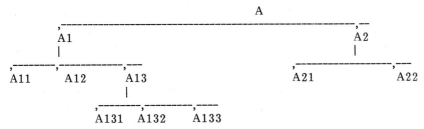

In this the children of person A are A1, A2, etc. The children of A2 are A21, A22, etc. A convenient search method for descendents is available in a database package or word processor if people are numbered this way. A search for the character string "A1" finds person A1 and all his descendents (A13, A131, etc).

It is sometimes convenient to number the generations. One system is to number the subject as generation 1, parents as 2, grandparents as 3, etc. Another system originated by Frank Leeson (Ref 8) allocates standard letters to people on the basis of the 30-year period in which they were born:

A	1380-1409	J	1650-1679	R	1890-1919
B	1410-1439	K	1680-1709	S	1920-1949
C	1440-1469	L	1710-1739	T	1950-1979
D	1470-1499	M	1740-1769	U	1980-2009
E	1500-1529	N	1770-1799	V	2010-2039
F	1530-1559	O	1800-1829	W	2040-2069
G	1560-1589	P	1830-1859	X	2070-2099
H	1590-1619	Q	1860-1889	Y	2100-2129
I	1620-1649			Z	2130-2159

This "Generation Grid" has an arbitrary datum at S for "Self", representing those now in full maturity. If pedigrees extend back before 1380, letters preceded by minus signs are used, working back from the –Z generation being 1350 to 1379. (That extension is not very convenient for computing, and I have not seen it used.)

In the system described below, Don Francis uses these letters to apply to the number of generations rather than the dates. S for "Subject", R for parents, Q for grandparents, etc.

DATABASE FOR FAMILY RECORDS

There are two approaches to using databases for linked family records, and I will describe one example of each. The first is the "family group" approach. In this, one record contains the names and vital dates of the father of a family, and some information about the mother, the marriage, and all the children. The other method is the "individual" approach. In this there is a separate record for each person; either this record or a marriage record shows the links to spouse, and parents or children.

EXAMPLE OF FAMILY GROUP METHOD

Don Francis (Ref 9,10,11) has used Vufile on both a Spectrum and a BBC micro for his own personal family history. The record format used was:

Ref-No	7 Characters: Generation letter, last 3 digits of year of birth, hyphen, one digit to show the branch of the family, finally 1 for male or 2 for female. Example P828-11 showing a great-grandparent, born 1828, branch 1 of the family, male.
Forenames	3-letter abbreviations
Birth Date	7 digits; year (without millenium), month and day numbers
Parish of birth	Abbreviated, usually 2 letters for county and 2 for parish
Death date	7 digits, eg 8741025 for 1874, October 25th.
Parish of death	Abbreviated, as parish of birth
Father	Reference number, surname, and abbreviated forenames
Mother	ditto
Spouse	ditto
Marriage date	As for birth, death date
Parish of marriage	As for parishes of birth, death
Heir	The child who is the link forward to the next generation in this pedigree.
Other children	Abbreviated forenames and last two digits of year of birth. An indicator shows which children are from which marriage.
Occupation	In brief
Other Information	Includes reference to will or census, also details of other marriages.

The generation letters are used to show the number of generations back from the subject on the basis of S for Self, R for parents, Q for grand-parents. As described above, this is a variant of the Leeson Letter (Ref 8) which is allocated in 30-year periods.

Vufile has variable length fields. Every field is present in every record, but if there is no information it only wastes one character. This feature allows common names and places to be abbreviated and save space, while uncommon names and places can be spelt out in full.

EXAMPLE OF INDIVIDUAL RECORD WITH LINKAGE

This is the system I have used for my own personal family history records. I have used a database called "Datawriter", initially on a Tandy Model 1. I have recently transferred the data on to a Tandy Model 4. I have described this system before in an article in "Computers in Genealogy" (Ref 1). To illustrate it I will use the family with my great-grandfather John Hawgood, his sister Matilda, and their parents Samuel and Louisa. There are six other children not shown. (This is the John Hawgood who moved in the 1890's to Bramber, Sussex, shown in the postcard on the front cover).

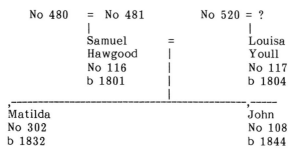

```
     No 480    =  No 481        No 520 = ?
               |                        |
               Samuel        =          Louisa
               Hawgood       |          Youll
               No 116        |          No 117
               b 1801        |          b 1804
                             |
        ,--------------------------------------------,-----
        Matilda                                      John
        No 302                                       No 108
        b 1832                                       b 1844
```

In a family history file we need a way of showing the links from children to parents. The way I provide this is to give every person a reference number, and a family reference formed from the reference numbers of the father and mother. In the example Matilda's reference is 302. Her father John is 116, her mother Louisa is 117, so Matilda's family reference is 116/117. Each family also has a marriage record, which contains the mother's reference number and forenames with her married surname, and also contains the family reference.

RECORD TYPE	PERSON REF	SURNAME	FORENAMES	BIRTH YEAR	FAMILY REF
M	117	Hawgood	Louisa	1804	116/117
P	302	Hawgood	Matilda	1832	116/117
P	108	Hawgood	John	1844	116/117
P	116	Hawgood	Samuel	1801	480/481
P	117	Youll	Louisa	1804	520/0

Family "116/117" includes the personal records (type P) for two children, Matilda and John, with the marriage record (type M) showing the mother with her married name, Louisa Hawgood. If the file is sorted by families, these are grouped together. Elsewhere in the file are the personal records for the father Samuel Hawgood (116) showing his parents as reference 480 and 481. Louisa appears with her maiden surname, Youll. I don't know anything about her mother, so this is shown as zero for "not yet known". This system works well for multiple marriages, illegitimate children, etc. I use reference 1 for unknown fathers of illegitimate children.

When I started putting these records into my computer, I only intended to create a summary for quick reference. As I use them more, I find that I want a larger proportion of my information included, and expand the records. However, the basic structure of my records has not changed. I have been able to add to it as my needs grow.

Some people make considerable use of abbreviations to fit more records into the space available, others are insistent on spelling all information out in full to make it easy to read. From my experience, I recommend a minimum use of abbreviations.

Opposite are examples of the two types of record in my database, "Personal" records and "Marriage" records.

PERSONAL RECORD

FIELD	TYPICAL CONTENTS
Reference	116
Record Type	P
Surname	Hawgood
Forenames	Samuel
Birthdate	18040617-
Birthplace	SRY Southwark, St Geo Martyr (bapt)
Marriage date	1832-
Marriage place	?
Death date	1871Q1
Death place	SSX Brighton
Family	480/481
Sources	C:pr, D:GROI, BD+BP+OC:cs51
Notes	Pawnbroker, Old Kent Rd

MARRIAGE RECORD

FIELD	TYPICAL CONTENTS
Reference	117
Record Type	M
Surname	Hawgood
Forenames	Louisa Weller
Birthdate	1804-5
Birthplace	SRY Southwark
Marriage date	1832-
Marriage place	?
Death date	18661008
Death place	HRT Sawbridgeworth
Family	116/117
Sources	M:b-cert of s Jn shows both surnames
Notes	nee Youll, m Samuel

Dates:

I allow up to 9 characters for dates. The first four are always a year in full (e.g. 1866). Where full information is available this is followed by two digits for month, and two for day. Dates shown in this way sort into correct chronological order. They can be followed by + for after, - for before, c for circa, ? for uncertain, and G if only the generation is known. Thus 18040617- shows "before 17th June 1804" (which is the known date of a baptism). If only the quarter is known, from General Registry Office indexes, the year is followed by Q1, Q2, Q3 or Q4. 1804-5 indicates a date in 1804 or 1805 - in this case calculated from the age given in the census.

Old Style Dates:

Before 1752 in England (and other years in other countries) the year number in legal dates changed on March 25th. Thus the day after 31st December 1688 was 1st January 1688, and the day after 24th March 1688 was 25th March 1689. This is shown by giving January, February, and March up to 24th the month numbers 13, 14 and 15. Thus the dates mentioned are 16881231, 16881301, 16881524, and 16890325.

Places:

In my system place fields start with the 3 letter Chapman County Code (Ref 12), e.g. SRY for Surrey and SSX for Sussex; this is followed by the place-name in full.

Sources:

To give a complete source for a fact, it is necessary to show which fact, what type of document, where I consulted the document (or a transcript or index), and who is the subject of the document. One method involves listing the sources in a separate numbered list, and referring to the source by its number in the list. Another method is to give the reference, possibly in abbreviated form, in the record with the fact it supports. I have used the latter approach, but as I have added more detail the abbreviations became unwieldy. I would now recommend anyone to start with a list of events and their sources, and cross refer to this in the personal family history database.

The system I have used is to abbreviate the elements of the source. The fact involved is shown by a tag, e.g. M for Marriage, BP for Birth Place, OC for Occupation. The type of document and transcript or index consulted are combined into one abbreviation - e.g. BOYD for Boyd's marriage index, GROI for the index at the General Registry Office in London, pr for Parish Register. If the subject of the source document is not the subject of the computer record, that information is added with the relationship and name abbreviated. For example, I have not found the record of the marriage of Samuel Hawgood and Louisa Weller Youll, but the birth certificate of their son John shows the mother's surname as "Hawgood formerly Youll", so I enter "b-cert of s Jn" as source of information for the marriage.

I have made this system for indicating sources progressively fuller, and more complex, as I have used my records. I find more and more that I want the source of each fact shown in my computer record.

Additional note on reference numbers:
Although the linkage system works if the reference numbers are allocated arbitrarily, I found it convenient to allocate numbers systematically to my first 30 ancestors. I use a modified version of the system described above in which 2 = father, 3 = mother, etc. My modification is to add 100 to the numbers: thus my father's reference is 102, my father's father's father John Hawgood is 108, his parents Samuel and Louisa are 116 and 117.

My personal family history database has changed more by increasing the amount of information about each person than by increasing the number of people mentioned. I have been able to do this without retyping any information – I have changed fields and added missing information.

Overall I have found that the database approach to keeping family history records is easy to start and can accomodate most of the information I want to have readily to hand.

DATABASES AND FAMILY TREES

In the next Chapter I describe the use of a word processor to print family trees. I have produced one family tree by moving a block of information about each person from a database to a word processor, then using the word processor to position the blocks of information in the correct place on the page. This was very time consuming with the software I was using, the Superscripsit word processor and Datawriter database on a Tandy, but would have been much easier on a word processor like Wordstar which allows one to move columns of information.
I have seen two other approaches to printing family trees from databases. Geoff Mather (Ref 13) uses Datastar on a Superbrain micro with CP/M. He extracts information fom the database into the correct positions on a sheet of paper to give a family tree. David Barnard (Ref 14) uses computer aided design techniques to lay out the structure of the tree.

REFERENCES

The journal "Computers in Genealogy" is abbreviated as "Comp in Gen"

Ref 1   D Hawgood, "Using the Datawriter database on a Tandy for family history", Comp in Gen 1, 9 Sept 84 p240.

Ref 2   D Francis, "Microl database on a Spectrum for parish register transcription", Comp in Gen 1, 3 Sept 83 p112

Ref 3   K Salkeld, "Using Quest database and Wordwise on the BBC micro", Comp in Gen 1, 8 June 84 p210). (Quest is available from the Advisory Unit for Computer Based Education, Endymion Road, Hatfield, Herts AL10 8AU; there are cassette, ROM and disk based versions.)

Ref 4   D Wilcocks, "Monumental Inscription indexing on a BBC computer with Masterfile", Comp in Gen 1, 9 Sept 84 p235

Ref 5   D Barnard, "Data structure for the BBC micro in genealogy", Comp in Gen 1, 5 Sept 83 p117

Ref 6   D Barnard, "Data structures for the BBC micro (II)", Comp in Gen 1, 6 Dec 83 p153

Ref 7   D Barnard, "Genealogy database system for BBC micros", Comp in Gen 1, 7 March 84 p200 (David Barnard's address is 3 Highbury Road, Hitchin, Herts)

Ref 8   F Leeson, "A standard generation-letter system", letter in Comp in Gen 1, 3, March 83, p76.

Ref 9   D Francis, "VU-FILE: Further details of use for genealogy", Comp in Gen 1, 4 Jun 83 p87 (describes use of Sinclair ZX81 and Spectrum computers)

Ref 10   D Francis, "VUFILE database on the BBC micro", Comp in Gen 1, 5 Sept 83 p112

Ref 11   D Francis, "Answers about BBC VUFILE", Comp in Gen 1, 7 March 84 p196

Ref 12   C R Chapman, "The Chapman County Codes", Family History News & Digest 2, 4, Autumn 1980 p154. Also given in Genealogists' Magazine, 20 3, Sept 1980 p200.

Ref 13   G Mather "The construction and easy modification of family trees produced from a computer database", Comp in Gen 1, 8 Jun 84 p224

Ref 14   D Barnard "GG-CAD: Computer Aided Design comes to Genealogy", Comp in Gen 1, 9 Sept 84 p255.

Other References describing use of Databases for Genealogy:

C J Adie, "Using the DBASEII system for genealogy", Comp in Gen 1, 2 Dec 82 p28

D Francis "Masterfile (for Spectrum)", Comp in Gen 1, 8 June 84 p218

D J Francis "Databases I have known and loved" Comp in Gen 2,2 Dec 85 p30. An excellent 12 page article reviewing database packages available for Sinclair Spectrum and BBC.

D W Jopling "Genealogy using the 'At Last' database on the Amstrad PCW8512" Comp in Gen 2,7 Mar 87 p171. A one name study with 3000 events filed.

D W Jopling "Drop line charts using 'At Last' with the 'Cracker' spreadsheet" Comp in Gen 2,8 p199. Data stored as in the previous reference, extracted for printing as a drop-line family tree.

Mrs C J Barnes "Sussex census returns 1851 - Transcription and index" Comp in Gen 2,6 Dec 86 p132. Using Caxton Cardbox on an Amstrad PCW, then indexing with DCS Indexer.

Mrs L Race "Commodore 64 - transcribing parish registers for the Society of Genealogists" Comp in Gen 2,2 p43. Use of Superbase, Vizawrite and Vizastar in transcription.

Mrs E Kenward, "Parish Register Indexing using Masterfile" Comp in Gen 2 ,6 p141. Describes programs in BASIC written to give a compact two-column index to a 1200 record transcript on a BBC micro.

D Hawgood "Computers and family history - a way to start" Family Tree 2, 6 Sep 86 p27. Field lengths and datatypes for Name, event, date, place, relation, notes.

D Hawgood "Computers and family history - how to set up a database" Family Tree 3,7 May 87 p15. Applying previous reference, using Digita "Datastore" on Amstrad PCW.

CHAPTER FIVE

WORD PROCESSING

THE COMPUTER AS A HELPFUL TYPEWRITER

A word processing package on a micro-computer is designed for the input, editing, storage, and printing of textual information. As text is typed in, it is first shown on the display, rather than being printed immediately as on a typewriter. The computer looks after line endings: if a word cannot be completed on a line, the entire word is moved down to the next line.

Text can be inserted or deleted. The document can be stored away on cassette or disk, and reloaded later for re-use. The whole or part of a document can be printed; line length, page length, line spacing, and similar parameters are chosen to suit the document.

Complete blocks of text can be moved around within a document, or to another document. It is also possible to make the computer search for a particular word or combination of characters, and if desired replace it by another throughout the document. For example it is possible to expand abbreviations.

To me, the great advantage of word processing is that it enables me to produce professional-looking typed documents, although I am by no means a good typist. I have made progressively more use of the fancier facilities available on word processors, but I derived much of the benefit of word processing using a very simple system.

There are three main uses for word processors in family history: typing documents to send to other people, record keeping particularly for descriptive matter, and the production and maintenance of family trees. I will not describe the first as there are many books on producing typed documents with word processors, but I will say a little about the other two uses.

KEEPING RECORDS WITH A WORD PROCESSOR

Using a word processor is an excellent way of storing miscellaneous pieces of descriptive family history, and transcripts of textual sources like wills and deeds. Keeping records as word processor documents is a cheap and easy approach, but it suffers from the disadvantage that the records cannot usually be sorted automatically. Searching for words or combinations of characters is very fast, but the search cannot be for combinations like "forename John and occupation maltster". However the search can be arranged to stop at every occurrence in the file of a set of characters, displaying a screenful of information at that point, then continue to the next occurrence by one keystroke. For example by choosing "maltster" as the search string, I can very quickly tap through the file looking at every place that word occurs.

One approach to keeping family history records on a word processor is to maintain them in the form in which they are distributed to other members of the family. For example, it is possible to keep a set of family group sheets, or a family history book, in the word processor. If more information is found, it can be added to the file. In this way the family book will always be up to date if a copy is printed.

In keeping miscellaneous pieces of information, I find it useful to start the note with an index line. This includes the reference number I have allocated, the name and dates, and a reference to the database file where further set information about this person is maintained. The note continues with the source reference of the information contained within it. For example:

D3241 Henry Jones 1732-1794 (File JONES2)
Will proved Archdeaconry court of Lewes 1795, now at East Sussex Record Office, Lewes, ref A77-341

Henry Jones index line could be expanded to include all the basic information about him:

D3241 Henry Jones b 25 May 1732 Parham SSX son of William Jones D324, m 15 June 1756 at Dartford KEN to Elizabeth White, d 1 Nov 1794 Brighton SSX
(I have invented this information about Henry Jones)

Some people keep extensive family records in this style. It has the advantage of simplicity, but the disadvantage that the manipulation possible within a word-processing package is quite limited.

This technique works well with logically-constructed reference numbers. If William Jones is D324 as "4th child of 2nd child of 3rd child of progenitor D", a search for the characters D324 will find him and all his descendants - his children D3241, D3242, D3243 etc and their children D32411, D32412, etc.

Word processing packages give facilities to mark the start and end of a selected part of a text, then move it or copy it to another part of the document. For example in writing a book I type references as I come to them, and move them all to the end of the chapter when it is finished. I have also used this for repeating entries in a list of map references under an alternative form of a parish name, so that the same entry appears for "Long Marston" and "Marston, Long" - I just copy the entry to the alternative alphabetical position in the list, then change the word order. It is very easy to keep a list in a "sensible" order using a word processor - for example putting "Saint" and "St" entries together. Even when you are well into computing, running databases and writing your own programs, you may find the quickest way to set up a small index is on a word processor.

On some systems it is possible to move information between database packages and word processor packages. I have moved information on my Tandy from the database Datawriter to the word-processor Super-Scripsit, and included it as a list in the middle of a textual family history. This is easier with "integrated" packages which usually include a database, a word processor, and a spreadsheet for financial calculations. The Sinclair QL, for example, has a set of integrated packages of this type.

PRINTING FAMILY TREES

I find the use of a word processor the best way of producing family trees in the conventional horizontal format, both for my own use and for sending to other members of the family. The figure overleaf shows a Lilburn family tree. I produced this with the Superscripsit word processor package on my Tandy, using a daisy wheel printer at 15 characters per inch.

There are two main problems in printing family trees. One is that the information to be included, and arrangement of the tree, depend on the purpose for preparing the tree. The other is that the paper is never wide enough for all the information we want to include. This problem is not peculiar to computers: we have all seen family trees drawn out on several sheets of paper pasted together. Getting as much as possible onto a family tree from a word processor is helped by having:

a wide printer;
small typeface;
display as a "window" on a wider text.

Wide printers cost more than narrow ones, so this is mainly a matter of what you can afford. However there is a trick available on some dot matrix printers. This is to print the letters sideways on a long strip of paper. For example, the back cover of "Computers in Genealogy" for March 1984 (Ref 1) is a family tree 88 letters wide produced from a printer which is only 32 letters wide. Norma Jennings produced this on a Sinclair Spectrum with a ZX printer and a word processor called "Shifty". A routine to accomplish this, using the same equipment, has been given by Alan Brennan (Ref 2). I used the same technique on my Amstrad PCW8512 using a program called "Rotate".

Most daisy wheel printers have 10 and 12 per inch typefaces available, some also have 15 or 16 per inch. Dot matrix printers usually have a condensed typeface of 16 per inch. It may also be possible to print in a typeface intended for subscripts and superscripts. Don Francis has used this with Wordwise and an Epson printer on a BBC micro (Ref 3). An example using the same combination is given by Keith Salkeld (Ref 4). If buying a system, make sure that the word processor package includes the controls needed to print with the small typeface, and allows enough characters on a line.

LILBURN FAMILY TREE (Prepared January 1985)

George
Lilburn
= Mary

John Lilburn
1779
b Nettleham Lincs
tailor
of Lincoln

Michael
Cass
brick-layer
of Malton
Yorks
=
Mary
Spavin
(1813)

Sarah Cass
1818
b Malton Yorks

William Lilburn
1815 - 1888
b Nettleham Lincs
Police Inspector
born and lived in Lincoln

Ann
= Robert
Robinson
of Ludford, Lincs

Susanna
Robinson
1805
b Ludford
Lincs
=
George
Taylor
1811
b New York nr Horncastle Lincs
road mender, of Spridlington Lincs

Robert
Taylor
1831
b Ingham
Lincs

George
Taylor
1847
b Spridlington
Lincs

Harriett Ann
Taylor
1841 - 1928
b Spridlington
Lincs
= (1867)

William Henry
Lilburn
1840 - 1929
b & lived in Lincoln
Sub-post-master

Jane
1838

George
1842

Hannah
1844

Charles Simpson
1846

Eliza
1848

Mary
1850

George
William
Lilburn
1869
b Lincoln

Susanna
Lilburn
1872 - 1944
b Lincoln
=
(1896)
William Bennet
Robinson
1870 - 1925
press artist,
Illustrated
London News

Harriett Ann
Lilburn
1874 - 1939
b Lincoln
= (1893)
Joseph Henry
Bowker
b Blackburn Lancs
Methodist minister
of Lancs, Yorks,
and London

Alice
Lilburn
c1879 - 1944
= Frederick
Myers

On some word processors lines of text wider than the display are wrapped round to occupy several successive lines on the display. This makes it very difficult to enter and edit a wide family tree, or any other wide table. It is easier to use a word processor on which "what you see is what you get". (This phrase is the origin of the dreadful jargon word "wysiwyg"). If the display acts as a window on a wider table of text, it is fairly easy to edit a wide family tree.

Another trick I have used on a printer with tractor feed is to print one family, then roll back the paper to the top of the page and print another family. For example I have used this in the tree below showing Excell sisters marrying Marshall cousins. This tree has a particular purpose, to show the connection between these two families (the Marshall family is distinguished in the Figure by grey tone, stuck on after the tree was printed). It therefore has information like William Marshall being Hezekiah Excell's executor, and their sons James Carver Excell and Thomas Marshall being partners in business, rather than the "standard" information on date and place of birth, marriage and death. This is another advantage of the word processor for producing family trees - you can include just the information needed for a particular purpose.

Excell-Marshall Relationship, Sussex and Wiltshire.

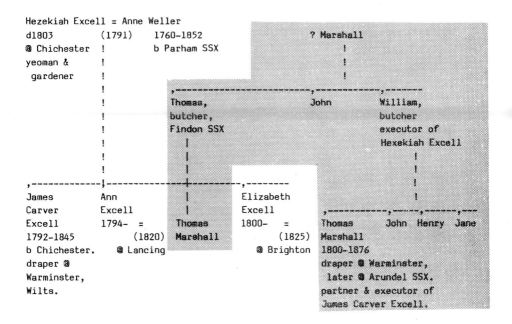

```
Hezekiah Excell = Anne Weller
d1803         (1791)    1760-1852                    ? Marshall
@ Chichester  !         b Parham SSX                     !
yeoman &      !                                           !
  gardener    !                                           !
              !         ,---------------------------,-------------,-------
              !         Thomas,                     John      William,
              !         butcher,                              butcher
              !         Findon SSX                            executor of
              !            |                                  Hexekiah Excell
              !            |                                      !
              !            |                                      !
,-------------!-----------,+--------,-------,---------            !
James       Ann           |        Elizabeth                     !
Carver      Excell        |        Excell          ,-----------,-----,------,---
Excell      1794-   =     |        1800-   =       Thomas    John Henry Jane
1792-1845        (1820)  Thomas          (1825)    Marshall
b Chichester. @ Lancing  Marshall        @ Brighton 1800-1876
draper @                                            draper @ Warminster,
Warminster,                                          later @ Arundel SSX.
Wilts.                                              partner & executor of
                                                    James Carver Excell.
```

NOTE ON SPREADSHEETS

For completeness, I will mention here that it is possible to use spreadsheet packages to produce family trees. I have not used this myself, but
it has been described by Althea Douglas (Ref 5) and Malcolm Smith (Ref
6). Althea Douglas used "Perfect Calc" on a Kaypro to produce columns
the same width for each person. Malcolm Smith used Vucalc on a Sinclair
Spectrum. His example shows the wide variation in the amount of
information we want to show about different people. He includes:

```
,---------,-------------------------------------,----------------,-------
John       William 12.2.1860-3.3.1950             Mary Ann         Elizabeth
1857-      biscuit factory watchman &             1862-            1864-
           Primitive Methodist Preacher
           of Reading
           m 10.11.1883 Mary Foster
           24.8.1860-14.12.1948 dau of
           Thomas & Sarah (Girdler) of
           Kingsclere, Hants
           All children born at Reading
```

REFERENCES:
(Comp in Gen is an abbreviation for "Computers in Genealogy").
Ref 1. N Jennings, Letter, "Family Tree from a Sinclair Spectrum", Comp
   in Gen 1, 7 March 84 p201
Ref 2. A Brennan, "Bits on the side: a 48K Spectrum utility to print
   family tree diagrams", Comp in Gen 1, 9 Sept 84 p245
Ref 3. D Francis, in "Notes and News": Tiny printing with an Epson
   printer on a BBC micro. Comp in Gen 1, 7 Mar 84 p171
Ref 4 K Salkeld "Using Quest database and Wordwise on the BBC micro",
   Comp in Gen 1, 8 Jun 84 p210)
Ref 5. A Douglas, "You use your spreadsheet for what?", Comp in Gen 1,
   6 Dec 83 p165.
Ref 6. M Smith, letter, "Vucalc spreadsheet for family trees", Comp in
   Gen 1, 9 Sept 84 p230

Other articles concerning use of word processing for genealogy:
M Wilshin, "Is your program strictly necessary", Comp in Gen 1, 4 Jun 83
   p80. Uses Wordstar on an Apple microcomputer with CP/M. There are
   some neat ideas in the layout of the family tree reproduced with this
   article.
D Francis, "Wordwise: a word processing package for the BBC micro",
   Comp in Gen 1, 6 Dec 83 p142.
J F Swan, letter, "Printing family trees", Comp in Gen 1, 8 Jun 84 p219.
   Gives an example of a family tree printed on a Tandy CGP115 printer,
   which is cheap and prints lines and characters clearly in four colours.
J Hitchon, "Producing family trees on a BBC micro", Comp in Gen 1, 9
   Sept 84 p248. A short program in BASIC is given which sets the
   function keys on a BBC micro using the word processor Wordwise to
   produce character strings like at+..........+, and set an Epson printer
   into condensed printing mode.

CHAPTER SIX

GENEALOGY PACKAGES

This chapter is mainly concerned with commercially available programs maintaining family relationships and pedigrees, storing the information on cassette tape or on disk. There is also a note on packages for census transcription and analysis.

A couple of years ago I wrote programs in Basic which had the same facilities as the simplest type of genealogy package. I could enter limited information about people. Then by selecting one person I could display the names and dates of their children, parents, and grand-parents. I showed these programs at Christmas at my wife's parents' home in New Zealand. The family found it interesting – the younger members were being shown information they had not seen before, the older members were volunteering extra information. I had been asked to show it because the family wanted to see what I was doing with computers, but it provoked a lively discussion of the history of the family.

This program was useful in providing and eliciting information, but it was not useful to me as a research tool in manipulating information. Conversely, I have found a database package to be an excellent research tool, but the lists of information it provides are not at all good for showing to other members of the family.

There are over fifty genealogy packages on sale in the U.S.A., with prices varying from $10 to $400. A list of them is published in the American journal "Genealogical Computing" every two months. Some are simple, providing a handy way of showing other people the results of research. Others aim to combine this function with those of a research tool. In effect these incorporate a database and a system of free text notes, with a system of identity numbers to link all the information together.

GENERAL DESCRIPTION OF GENEALOGY PACKAGES

All the packages and programs store information about a collection of named persons. Each person has either a reference number or a position in a structure. Relationship to other people in the collection is shown either by using their reference numbers, or by their position in the same data structure. Other information about people in the collection will include dates and places of vital events, and may include names and information for other people who do not have prime records.

Packages vary enormously in scope and complexity. The simplest deal with direct ancestors only, often up to great-great-grandparents of the subject with a total of 30 ancestors. These may allow for all the other children of these ancestors, with their spouses, so the total number of people in even a simple package may be several hundred. But the structure depends on the direct ancestors; there is no way to enter information about cousins, or people with the same surname but no known relationship. Other packages allow entry of information about any person and can show relationship to any other person, linking children to parents and husbands to wives through reference numbers. Many of the packages provide only preset information fields, usually the date and place of birth, marriage and death. More complex ones allow the genealogist to define fields to be included, provide several fields for notes and sources, or provide a cross-reference to a separate file of free text information about each person.

Certain types of printed output are available in most packages:

Family Group Sheet: An example printed by "Family Roots" is shown in Figure 1 opposite. This type of output, with information about a couple and their children, is available in most of the packages. The amount of information available about each person varies from package to package.

Ancestor Chart or Birth Brief: Most of the packages produce this type of chart. Some have options of showing all direct ancestors for 4 generations, or of showing more generations following either the male line throughout or female line throughout.

Descendent Chart or Indented Family Tree: This type of vertical arrangement of family tree is available in some of the packages. The amount of information per person varies. I consider that these work best with all information for two or three generations. I find them confusing if the number of generations is increased. Figure 2 is an example printed from "Family Roots". The top part of the figure uses an option to print names only. Alternatively full information can be printed for each person, as shown at the bottom of the figure.

Sorted lists are available in most packages. In some lists in reference number or birth date order only are available, in others you can choose to sort by forename, surname, married surname, place or date of birth marriage or death, and other fields you choose. Furthermore, they allow the records included in the list to be selected. Such combinations as "Born before 1837 in Sussex" or "Forename Henry or Harry" may be available. These facilities become very similar to those of database packages as described in Chapter 4.

PACKAGES WITH FAMILY LINKS

The three top selling American packages are Family Roots, Personal Ancestral File, and Roots 2. All of these hold full information about people, marriages, and information sources. Reports printed are well formatted, suitable to send to other family members. All can accept data in the standard GEDCOM format, Personal Ancestral File can generate data in GEDCOM format.

Figure 1   Genealogy Packages 49

HUSBAND: William Henry Lilburn (ID=14)
Born 07 Feb 1840   Place Lincoln LIN
Marr 05 Aug 1867   Place St Nicholas Lincoln LIN
Died 25 Feb 1929   Place 3 Bailgate Lincoln LIN
HUSBAND'S
FATHER: William Lilburn (ID=28)   HUSBAND'S
                                         MOTHER: Sarah Cass (ID=29)
OTHER WIVES:

WIFE: Harriett Ann Taylor (ID=15)
Born 11 Apr 1841   Place Spridlington LIN
Died 20 Mar 1928   Place Lincoln LIN
WIFE'S
FATHER: George Taylor (ID=30)   WIFE'S
                                       MOTHER: Susannah Robinson (ID=31)
OTHER HUSBANDS:

M/F	CHILDREN	WHEN BORN	WHERE BORN	FIRST MARRIAGE	WHEN DIED
1 M	George William Lilburn (ID=149)	11 Aug 1869	93 Bailgate Lincoln LIN	1896 William Bennet Robinson (ID=151)	?? Oct 1944
2 F	Susanna Lilburn (ID=150)	19 Jul 1872	Lincoln LIN	1893 Joseph Henry Bowker Rev. (ID=6)	1939
3 F	Harriett Ann Lilburn (ID=7)	03 Aug 1874	93 Bailgate Lincoln LIN	1904c Frederick Myers (ID=153)	?? Aug 1944
4 F	Alice Lilburn (ID=152)	14 Apr 187?	Lincoln LIN		

SOURCES OF INFORMATION   OTHER MARRIAGES

Bapt cert
D cert
M cert
1841 Census West Bight Lincoln
Family info - Alison Hawgood
Birthday book of Alison Hawgood
B cert
1871 Census 93 Bailgate Lincoln LIN
Family info - Barbara Foxon
Family info (Alan Hawgood)

Figure 2

```
DESCENDANTS OF Richard Sapp   (ID=210)            18/1/85


                             GREAT
                    GRAND    GRAND
PERSON    CHILDREN  CHILDREN CHILDREN
!         !         !        !
!Richard Sapp (ID=210)
!         !
!         !Richard Sapp (ID=207)
!         !    MOTHER: Elizabeth @Sapp (ID=255)
!         !
!         !John Sapp (ID=208)
!         !    MOTHER: Elizabeth @Sapp (ID=255)
!         !    !
!         !    !John Sapp (ID=203)
!         !    !   MOTHER: Elizabeth Float (ID=216)
!         !    !
!         !    !Elizabeth Sapp (ID=204)
!         !    !   MOTHER: Elizabeth Float (ID=216)
!         !    !
!         !    !John Sapp (ID=205)
!         !    !   MOTHER: Elizabeth Float (ID=216)
!         !    !
!         !    !Richard Sapp - (ID=80)
!         !    !   MOTHER: Elizabeth Float (ID=216)
!         !    !   !
!         !    !   !Elizabeth Sapp (ID=199)
!         !    !   !   MOTHER: Elizabeth White . (ID=81)
!         !    !   !
!         !    !   !Richard Sapp (ID=200)
!         !    !   !   MOTHER: Elizabeth White . (ID=81) ___
!         !    !   !
!         !    !   !John Sapp (ID=40)
!         !    !   !   MOTHER: Elizabeth White . (ID=81)
!         !    !   !
!         !    !   !Peter Sapp (ID=202)
!         !    !   !   MOTHER: Elizabeth White . (ID=81)
!         !
!         !Peter Sapp (ID=239)
!         !    MOTHER: Elizabeth @Sapp (ID=255)
!         !
!         !Susan Sapp (ID=209)
!         !    MOTHER: Elizabeth @Sapp (ID=255)
!         !    !
!         !    !John Kinch (ID=245)
!         !    !   FATHER: Thomas Kinch (ID=217)
```

```
!Richard Sapp (ID=200)
!    B: 05 Jan 1765*1 @ Walberton SSX
!    M: 05 May 1789*3 to Sarah Rusbridger (ID=213) @ Walberton SSX
!    SEX: M
!    OCC: Gamekeeper*2
!    LIV: Boxgrove SSX*2
!    (1: bapt PR)
!    (2: 1806 Conveyance in WSRO)
!    (3: PR)
!    2 Children
!    MOTHER: Elizabeth White . (ID=81)
```

Personal Ancestral File has been produced by the Genealogical Department of the Church of Jesus Christ of Latter Day Saints. It is very good value. It has been produced by the Mormons as a service to members of their church and others interested in genealogy, rather than as a profit-making venture. It has two parts. One is a lineage-linked subsystem. Places and dates of birth/baptism, marriage, death and burial together with names and titles of the person are recorded. For LDS members, ordinance dates and places can be entered. Linkages to parents, spouses, and children are included. History notes about each person can be used for source references or additional information. This part of the package provides pedigree and family group charts. The other part is the data sort utility, intended for the entry and organisation of transcripts and sources of original information. This section is a research tool, allowing searching and sorting in a variety of ways. For reviews and description see Ref 1. Personal Ancestral File is available for IBM PC compatibles, for Apple 2, and for micros with CP/M in Kaypro format, from The Church of Jesus Christ of Latter Day Saints, either at 751 Warwick Road, Solihull, West Midlands B91 3DQ, phone 021-705-6731, or at Salt Lake Distribution Centre, 1999 West 1700 South, Salt Lake City, Utah 84104, USA. Price is $35.00 or its equivalent (currently about £20). Versions in other formats are available from independent software suppliers. One such is the Amstrad PCW version available at £59 from Kintech Computers, St Tudy, Bodmin, Cornwall PL30 3RH - phone 0208-850176.

Family Roots for PC compatibles, Apple II and Macintosh, selected CP/M systems (not Amstrad PCW), Commodore 64 and 128. I used this to produce figures 1 and 2. Basic fields for forenames, surname, title, with date and place of birth marriage and death are pre-defined, but additional fields can be defined by the user. Footnotes can be added, with a cross-reference from any other field. This provides a good way of including source references. Additional longer text notes can be kept in a separate file, using the identity number to link it to the main file. I am impressed by the package: it seemed to be suitable both as a research tool and for communicating the results of research. For reviews etc see Ref 2. Available from its publishers, Quinsept Inc, PO Box 216, Lexington MA 02173 USA (617-641-2930) at $185, can also be ordered from Michael Gurr Associates, 140 High St, Tenterden, Kent TN30 6HT (05806-4278) at £171.

Roots 2 runs on IBM PC and compatibles. "Roots/M" is an earlier version for microcomputers with CP/M. This package condenses names and places, and holds limited information per person, so it packs more people onto a disk. Searches can be made for similar-sounding surnames, using the Soundex code. On Roots 2 you can display a family tree, and browse through the family. For reviews see Ref 3. Roots 2 is published by Commsoft Inc, 2257 Old Middlefield Way, Mountain View, CA 94043 USA (415-967-1900) at $195. Roots/M for CP/M micros (not Amstrad PCW) is $49.95. Either can be ordered through Michael Gurr Associates at £195, £57 respectively (address see Family Roots).

BRITISH LINEAGE-LINKED PACKAGES

Three British packages are well-established but comparatively limited. Any individuals can be entered, and linked to others. Names and dates are held in full, but provision for places and sources is restricted. Printed reports may lack headings and detail. These three are Belgen, Genny and Easytree. BelGen is no longer in production, being replaced by Heritage.

Genny for PC compatibles, Amstrad PCW and Amstrad CPC from DCS, 38 South Parade, Bramhall, Stockport SK7 3BJ (061-439 4841). Price is £35, or £27 to member of any Family History Society. Data is condensed, to hold up to 1000 people on a disk. On PCW, dates are year only. It can hold 5 lines of notes per person, 10 lines on the Amstrad PCW version. Review, see Ref 4.

Belgen was produced for BBC micros and cassette version for Spectrum by Beltech Ltd, College House, St Leonards Close, Bridgnorth, Shropshire WV16 4EW. The cassette version holds a limited amount of information - for example there is provision for date of birth and death, but not date of marriage. Review, see Ref 5. The disk version was enhanced to hold substantially more information. Pedigree and similar charts can be printed.

Easytree by Murray Kennedy (Galaxy Software) holds 300 people on BBC model B, 600 on BBC Master, with place and date of birth, marriage and death, also relationships. It can be used with disk or cassette. Birth briefs and descendant charts can be printed. The family trees printed have descendants in a column on the left, their ancestors to the right. I find this much easier to follow than an indented list. New reports are still being added - for example a list of people with father, mother and spouse of each is a very useful summary. There are good facilities for browsing up and down a family tree, also a GEDCOM data transfer program. Review and description, see Ref 6. Easytree for BBC computers, £19.95 (£29.95 on Archimedes, which gives 3500 person capacity) from Micro Aid, 25 Fore Street, Praze, Camborne, Cornwall TR14 0JX (0209-831274).

Two British packages are just being produced with much enhanced facilities, similar to those of the top American packages. Heritage, to a specification from the Society of Genealogists, has been written by David Lane, author of Belgen, and can read Belgen data. Pedigree is by Galaxy Software, who produced Easytree. Both have user defined variable-length fields and can hold information about tens of thousands of people, rather than hundreds in the earlier programs. Both will have GEDCOM data utilities for transfer of data to and from other packages.

Pedigree for PC compatibles, available November 1987 at £40 from Galaxy Software, 123 Links Drive, Solihull B91 2DJ (021 704 2839). Available later for Amstrad PCW. There are no pre-defined fields in this package: you can define whether each field is a date, text, or a linkage to other records. Screen layouts for data entry and display can be chosen by the user, so can report layouts. In Pedigree you can split the screen into several windows showing different displays. For example one can show a summary list, while another shows details for one person.

Heritage for BBC computers, £30, now (Nov 87) on system trial, to be available from Society of Genealogists, 14 Charterhouse Buildings, London EC1M 7BA (01-251 8799). It will be available for PC compatibles later. Description, see Ref 7. It has 10 pre-defined fields. These give names, lifespan, sex, father, mother, spouse(s), marriage dates, children. You can choose up to 22 other fields: for example these can include birth and death date, place, and source, occupation, residence, other sources, notes. There can be up to 2000 characters of information for a person. Dates allow for the "old style" with New Year at March 25th, for English Scottish or Continental dates. Qualifications of 'before', 'after' and 'circa' can be added. A good feature is the ability to show a summary index of names and lifespans on the screen while entering data, and use the index for identifying relatives.   Charts printed include birth briefs and family trees. Tables can be defined by the user, with sorting on three fields.

Two other packages have been introduced recently:

DAFT (Draw A Family Tree) for BBC micros. Dates, places and notes for people are entered in a database. Each A4 sheet of their family trees is laid out as a separate file, then the trees are printed. DAFT is £12 from John Hodges, 3 Arkwright Road, Milton Ernest, Bedford MK44 1SE (0232 5334). Review, see Ref 8.

Progen for Sinclair Spectrum (Cassette only), £7.50 from A. Biggs, (Gensoft), 70 Nelson Road, Ipswich, Suffolk, IP4 4DT. Each file holds data on a subject and four generations of direct ancestors, with space for their other children and spouses of those children.

PUBLIC DOMAIN SOFTWARE AND SHAREWARE

A number of American packages for PC compatibles are available through user groups. These are sold initially for a few pounds, with programs and documentation on the disk. If you like the program you register with the software publisher, paying about $40, and receive an up to date version of the program and notification of future upgrades. "Genealogy on display", "FT-ETC" and "Family Ties" have specifications near those of the top American programs. For Reviews of these programs see Ref 9.

Public Domain Software Library, Winscombe House, Beacon Road, Crowborough, Sussex TN6 1UL (08296-63298) supply FT-ETC as disk US2 460, Genealogy on Display version 4 as disk US1 218, Family Ties as disk US2 685. This library costs £14 to join then about £4.70 per disk, or £5.30 per disk for non-members. You may need earlier disks with more documentation, and may need a disk with a suitable version of BASIC.

IBM PC User Group, PO Box 830, London SE1 0BD (01-620-2244, but its better to write) supply Genealogy on display (disk PCUSG 220) and FT-ETC (disk PCUSG 126a). This group is £23 to join, then £5 per disk.

Genealogy on display is by Melvin O Duke, PO Box 20836, San Jose, CA 95160 USA (408-268-6637), about $45.

FT-ETC is $35 from Pine Cone Software, PO Box 1163, Columbus IN 47202 USA.

Family Ties is by Computer Services, 1050 East 800 South, Provo, Utah 84601 USA, and costs $55.

GENEALOGY DATABASES WITHOUT FAMILY LINKAGE

GG-5 This program for BBC micros is an enhancement of GG-3 described on page 31. It can now handle files spanning several disks. It is available from its author David Barnard, 3 Highbury Road, Hitchin, Herts (0462-50564). Description, see Ref 10.

Micro-CODIL This is a sophisticated package by Chris Reynolds of Brunel University. It includes fuzzy matching, handles text and approximate information. For description of the mainframe version CODIL, see Ref 11. MicroCODIL Family History Pack for BBC Master includes sample databases of genealogical and historical data. It is £40 from CODIL language systems, 33 Buckingham Road, Tring, Herts HP23 4HS.

Genbase This is a very simple database for information about individual recorded events, with preset fields for name, father, mother, date and notes. It can produce inverted records - e.g. entering a marriage produces two records, one with the husband as principal and the other with wife as principal. Genbase for PC compatibles, Amstrad PCW, Amstrad CPC, from DCS (see Genny), £25, or £20 to members of Family History Societies. Review, see Ref 12.

Marriage Index This is an even simpler databases for marriage information from parish registers. There are preset fields for two names, the date, and a three-character abbreviation of the parish name. It produces additional inverted records as for Genbase. It is available for Amstrad PCW from DCS (see Genny), £15. Review, see Ref 13.

Genealogical software Various databases, (e.g Masterfile by Campbell Systems) with fields preset for Genealogy. Sinclair Spectrum and Amstrad CPC464, from £14.95. Genealogical Software, 12 The Grove, West Wickham, Kent BR4 9JS.

DATA TRANSFER STANDARDS: GEDCOM and AGCI

All the different genealogy packages have their own formats for data. You cannot take your Personal Ancestral File data disk and read it with Family Roots. What you can do is to make a copy of the Personal Ancestral File data, transferring it to a common standard called GEDCOM, then transfer it from GEDCOM into Family Roots format. In the same way, data from Easytree can be transferred to Personal Ancestral File with GEDCOM as intermediary. GEDCOM stands for Genealogical Data Communications. The standard has been developed by the Church of Jesus Christ of Latter Day Saints, to provide a way of transferring data between different computer systems. GEDCOM formats can hold a very wide range of genealogical information. This is done by putting each piece of information such as a date, place or name in its own record, together with a tag showing what type of information, also a level number and cross reference showing what other piece of information it refers to. For information on GEDCOM see Ref 15.

AGCI (Australasian Genealogical Computer Index) is a very different data standard. Originating with the Society of Australian Genealogists, it is intended for collecting a central index of information from a number of different record offices and libraries. AGCI uses a few fixed length fields to hold a standard set of information about an event: name of principal, event, date, place, source type, source reference. Once a line is entered, it is very easy to merge it with others and print it on microfiche. See Ref 16.

REFERENCES

Comp in Gen is an abbreviation for "Computers in Genealogy"

Ref 1. P Andereck, "Personal Ancestral File Part 1 - Data fields, menus, and program files", Genealogical Computing 3, 6 May 84 p4, and "Personal Ancestral File part 2 - Data Sort Utility" Genealogical Computing 4,1 July 84 p6. C J Bradish, "Review: Personal Ancestral File Program (PAF)" Comp in Gen 2,6 p126. Also see Ref 14, p235.

Ref 2. P Andereck, "The genealogy software to beat", Genealogical Computing 4,2 Sept 84 p1, and "Family Roots going forward on all fronts" Genealogical Computing 6, 3 Mar 87 p1. Also Ref 14 p103.

Ref 3. J Bussell, "Review of Commsoft's Package Roots/M", Comp in Gen 1, 7 March 84 p198. P. Andereck, "Commsoft's Roots II Changes" Genealogical Computing, 5, 2 Dec 85 p4. Also Ref 14 p225

Ref 4. D Hawgood, "Genny", Comp in Gen, 2,4 Mar 86 p77

Ref 5. D Francis, "Beltech genealogy package", Comp in Gen 1, 8 June 1984 p215

Ref 6. D Francis, review of Easytree, Comp in Gen 1, 12 June 1985 p345. M Kennedy, "Easytree" Comp in Gen 1, 12 June 1985 p334.

Ref 7. D Francis, "Heritage", Comp in Gen 2,7 Mar 87 p 165

Ref 8. M Miller, "DAFT - a package to produce family trees", Comp in Gen 2,7 Mar 87 p185

Ref 9. Articles and letters in Computers in Genealogy, all called "Public Domain Software" (or variants of that). M Y Hillman, Sept 86 p113. H A Rydings, Dec 86 p149. C Essery, June 87 p204. S.Hayes, Sept 87 p243.

Ref 10. D Barnard, "GG-5, a large capacity database for BBC micros", Comp in Gen 2,4 June 86 p84.

Ref 11. C F Reynolds, "Considerations in the design of a genealogical database", Comp in Gen 1,1 p2

Ref 12. D Hawgood, "Genbase - an event filing package", Family Tree 3,5 Mar 87 p13.

Ref 13. Mrs C J Barnes, "Marriage Index", Comp in Gen 2,6 Dec 86 p128

Ref 14. P Andereck & R Pence, "Computer Genealogy" Ancestry Publishing, Salt Lake City, 1985.

Ref 15. D Hawgood, "Update on GEDCOM" Comp in Gen 2,4 Jun 86 p90

Ref 16. N Vine-Hall, "Australasian Genealogical Computer Index", Descent 15, 2 Jun 1985. Also D Hawgood, "Australasian Genealogical Computer Index AGCI" Comp in Gen 2,4 Jun 86 p88

APPENDIX ONE   COMPUTERS PEOPLE USE

Prices and computer models in the shops change very fast. This makes it very difficult to recommend what to buy. However I can list some machines which have been used in genealogy, with approximate current prices. You should check for yourself the price and capabilities of equipment you are buying. At present the Amstrad PCW and a variety of machines compatible with the IBM PC (e.g. Tandy 1000, Tandon, Amstrad PC1512) are the best buys for genealogy. In choosing computers, software is as important as hardware, so the two have to be considered together.

Discounts are available from user groups, High Street multiple stores, and mail order suppliers. There is a definite advantage in buying from someone who will provide support and maintenance, particularly when you first start computing. If at all possible see your computer assembled and working in the shop before you take it home. If this is not possible, go through the operations of turning on the machine and loading the software on an identical machine.

It is worth buying home computer magazines when deciding what to buy - see Appendix 2 for some titles. It is also worth visiting computer exhibitions. Although they are often very crowded it is useful to talk directly to suppliers, and see demonstrations of equipment and software. Articles in Which? magazine (e.g. November 1987) are very helpful, but remember when reading them that you need a printer and good database software, don't need good BASIC, games, graphics or sound.

In the U.K. the BBC micro and the Sinclair Spectrum were the most popular computers for use in genealogy; the Amstrad PCW and various IBM PC compatibles are catching them rapidly. With reduced prices for disk systems, there is now little use of cassette tape. In the USA, the Apple II, Tandy models 1/3/4, and IBM PC were most popular; PC compatibles are most popular now.

In looking at prices, bear in mind that the Sinclair, BBC, Atari and Commodore machines can use a domestic television set for display. However, most people who do much computing at home end up buying either a portable TV to go with the computer, or a monitor. A coloured medium resolution monitor is about £200, a green or amber screen monitor is about £75. As well as freeing the domestic TV for use by other members of the family, the better picture on a monitor is more restful on the eyes.

I have given a nominal figure for the amount of semi-conductor store, but the amount available for programs may be very much less. On 8 bit micros like the Spectrum, BBC, Apple II, Tandy model 4, and Amstrad PCW tricks like 'bank switching' and 'RAM disks' must be used if the store is over 64K. The Sinclair QL and IBM PC compatibles are 16 bit micros, so the store can be extended further.

For Sinclair, BBC, Apple, IBM and Amstrad there are numerous additions available from suppliers independent of their manufacturers. Many of these are excellent, but if you have a system composed of a variety of parts from different suppliers it may be more difficult to pin down someone to get the system working. You may be in a better position to use a mixed system if you have a "consultant" on hand - for example a spouse or child with experience of computers.

SINCLAIR: The Spectrum has been a popular home computer for genealogy in the U.K. Storage is on cassette, Sinclair microdrives, or disk. Store 128K. Spectrum 128k+2 with cassette is £150, Spectrum 128k+3 with disk is £200. A good selection of software is available, much of it from independent software houses. Databases worthy of note are Psion Vufile and Campbells Masterfile (£15). Both are economical in space as they use variable length fields. Masterfile has more facilities. Tasword is a good word processor. Since Amstrad bought the company, the Spectrum is being promoted more for games than databases and word processing.

The QL had a promising specification, with two microdrives and four software packages, including word processor and database, in the basic package. But it did not sell well, and is out of production.

COMMODORE 64 and 128 : very competitive with the Sinclair Spectrum. Much software has been transferred from the Commodore Pet, so there is a variety of database and word processing packages. Store is 64K, or 128K on the Commodore 128.   Price about £180 with cassette recorder, disk £150 extra. One good database is Superbase 64 from Precision Software (£100).

BBC Master from ACORN COMPUTERS: The predecessor, the 32K model 'B' is the most popular micro-computer in terms of numbers used by subscribers to "Computers in Genealogy". These have been popular with programmers, and widely used in U.K. schools. Store is 128K on Master. Price with a disk drive from £415 (Master Compact). There is a variety of software available, some of it as plug-in ROM modules. Word processors include View from Acornsoft (£60) (included as standard on later models) and Wordwise from Computer Concepts (£46), both in ROM. Masterfile from Beebugsoft (part of the BBC users group) is the most popular database for genealogy. For an excellent review of databases for BBC (and Spectrum) see "Databases I have known and loved" by Don Francis, Computers in Genealogy Dec 85 p30. Acorn have now produced a fast new machine, the Archimedes (from £980) compatible with the Master and B.

TANDY used to have their own designs, but now make IBM compatibles.

APPLE. Model II was popular, but Apple now concentrate on the Macintosh which is particularly good for desk top publishing, very expensive for genealogy.

IBM: PC (about £1700) These, and compatible machines, are the best selling personal computers for business, and are becoming widely used as home micros.   Store from 128K. The operating system is PCDOS or similar MSDOS. There is a vast range of software available; this used to be expensive - several hundred pounds for a word processing package or database. But there are now many packages available from £50. There are many IBM-compatible micros from other manufacturers, prices from £500 with disks. IBM have introduced a new Personal System/2: this is becoming important for business use, but I expect IBM PC compatibles to be available for many years.

AMSTRAD PCW very good value for money, complete with monitor, disk, printer and Locoscript word processing program. They run the standard operating system CP/M so there is a good variety of software available. PCW8256 at £344 has 256k and one disk drive, PCW8512 at £459 has 512k and two disk drives. Both these have a dot matrix printer. PCW9512 at £574 has 512k, one disk drive, and a daisy wheel printer. Suitable databases are At Last (which has better provision than most for dates before 1900), Campbells Masterfile (pleasant to use) and DBASEII (very flexible, but rather complicated to use). CPC6128 (£250) also runs CP/M, may be better if you want to choose your own printer. Amstrad PC1512 is compatible with the IBM PC. With twin floppy disks it is £574, up to £1034 with a 20 megabyte hard disk and a colour monitor. The PC1640 has 640k store and better screen resolution.

ATARI 520 from £300. Technically advanced and cheap, but short of genealogy and database software.

APPENDIX TWO: FURTHER READING, CLUBS, AND USEFUL ADDRESSES

BOOKS

P Andereck & R Pence, "Computer Genealogy – a guide to research through high technology" Ancestry Publishing, PO Box 476, Salt Lake City, Utah 84110 USA. 1985. 294 pages. Substantial descriptions of American genealogical packages and the GEDCOM data transfer standard.

Jan Worthington, "Computers for Genealogy", published by the author, P.O.Box 161, Lane Cove, Sydney 2066, Australia. 64 pages. 2nd edition, 1985. Lists and compares American and Australian genealogy packages, describes Australian transcription projects.

Sue Edgington, "Micro–history: Local history and computing projects" Hodder & Stoughton 1985, 60 pages. Aimed at school use of computers for population history. Lists 12 programs in BASIC.

British Computer Society, A glossary of computing terms – an introduction Cambridge University Press, 5th Edition 1987 (general edition £1.95, student's edition £1.65). Previous editions of the glossary have been concise, carefully constructed, and very useful.

International Federation for Information Processing, Elements of information and information processing for teachers in secondary schools, IFIP, 1976. and Computer education for teachers in secondary schools: Analysis and Algorithms, IFIP, 1977. The IFIP pamphlets are available from the British Computer Society, 13 Mansfield St, London W1. They are an excellent general introduction to the way information and its manipulation are viewed if they are to be handled by computer.

R Bradbeer, The Personal Computer Book, Gower Publishing Co Ltd, 2nd Edition, 1982. One of the best of the introductions to home computers, with a good bibliography.

R Bradbeer, P de Bono & P Laurie, The Computer Book, BBC 1982. This book accompanied a BBC television series on computers. It is a general introduction, not specifically about the BBC micro.

L R Carter & E Huzan, Computers and their Use, Teach Yourself Books, Hodder & Stoughton, 1984. A good introduction to computers in general, not aimed specifically at the home computer user.

E C Oliver & R Chapman, Data processing, DP Publications, 5th Edn 1981. Written as an introductory text for computing in business and accountancy, very sound and clear on the principles of data processing.

R Floud, An Introduction to quantitative methods for historians, Methuen 1973. This is an Open University set book. It is not a computing book, but is very well worth while reading if you want to make any statistical analysis of your information.

E A Wrigley (ed), Identifying People in the Past, Edward Arnold 1973. This book has a lot of information about record linkage by computer, with a good bibliography.

MAGAZINES

"Computers in Genealogy" is full of useful information and practical experience, and gives details of forthcoming meetings and courses in this field. As I edited this magazine for four years, I may be prejudiced, but I have find the articles very helpful to me. The subscription is £5 per annum for 4 issues, £4 for members of the Society of Genealogists or British Computer Society. Back issues are available. Published by the Society of Genealogists, 14 Charterhouse Buildings, London EC1M 7BA (phone 01-251 8799)

"Genealogical Computing" is an excellent journal edited by Paul Andereck and published every three months by Ancestry Publishing, PO Box 476, Salt Lake City, Utah 84110, USA. Annual subscription is $25 in USA, $30 Canada, $35 elsewhere. It has general articles and in particular details of genealogy packages; also good on data transfer standards.

"Personal Computer World" and "Practical Computing" are probably the two best general magazines in the home computer field; the former is very comprehensive, and has information about computer clubs and user groups. Practical Computing has very good surveys. Both of these are quite hard to understand if you are just starting to look at computers. There are other magazines which aim more at people without knowledge of computers: the best suggestion is to look at a few on a news-stand and buy one you can understand.

"Family Tree" (monthly on news-stands £1.15 or from 141 Great Whyte, Ramsey, Huntingdon, Cambs PE17 1HP (0487-814050) frequently has computer articles - authors include me and Colin Forrester.

COMPUTER USER GROUPS.

It is worth joining the user group for the make of computer you have bought, or are considering. Most are independent of the manufacturers, and their magazines give information about faults and difficulties. Many provide discounts on equipment and commercial computer programs, and have a library of free computer programs written by members. They are listed about every six months in "Personal Computer World", or addresses can be obtained by sending an sae to John Dale, Association of Computer Clubs, 12 Poplar Road, Newtown, Powys SY16 2QG

Two goups currently have meetings on the application of computers to genealogy. Meetings of the Computer Interest Group of the Society of Genealogists are held in London: details are given in the magazine "Computers in Genealogy", or can be obtained from the Society of Genealogists, see above. They are also in "Computing". This group is affiliated to the British Computer Society. The Birmingham and Midland Genealogy and Heraldry Society has a computer branch, meeting in Birmingham. For details contact John Fletcher, 4 Wellman Croft, Selly Oak, Birmingham B29 6NP (phone 021-472 6686).

FAMILY HISTORY SOCIETIES

There are family history societies covering every county of the United Kingdom. Details can be obtained by sending a stamped addressed envelope to Mrs P Saul, Administrator, Federation of Family History Societies, 31 Seven Star Road, Solihull, West Midlands B91 2BZ. Many Societies outside the UK are also affiliated to this Federation.

The Society of Genealogists, 14 Charterhouse Buildings, London EC1M 7BA has a library with a notable collection of copies of parish registers and other genealogical records. It is available to non-members on payment of search fees. Relevant publications are on sale, including those of the Society, and of the Federation of Family History Societies.

DATA PROTECTION

The Data Protection Registrar and Registry are at Springfield House, Water Lane, Wilmslow, Cheshire SK9 5AX. The Society of Genealogists has published an informative and practical leaflet "The Data Protection Act and Genealogists", 6 pages, price 20p plus 25p post & packing.

SOME SOFTWARE SUPPLIERS

Advisory Unit for Computer Based Education, Endymion Rd, Hatfield,
    Herts AL10 8AU.
David Barnard, 3 Highbury Rd, Hitchin, Herts. Phone 0462-50564.
Beebugsoft, PO Box 109, High Wycombe, Bucks HP11 2TD
Beltech Ltd, College House, St Leonards Close, Bridgnorth,
    Shropshire WV16 4EW. Phone 07462-5420.
Campbell Systems, 57 Trap's Hill, Loughton, Essex. Phone 01-508 5058.
Computer Concepts, Gaddesden Place, Hemel Hempstead, Herts HP2 6EX.
    Phone 0442-63933.
Precision Software, 6 Park Terrace, Worcester Park, Surrey KT4 7JZ.
    Phone 01-330 7166.

(Suppliers of Genealogy Packages are listed in Chapter 6.)

GLOSSARY

Computing is bedevilled by jargon, and by different people using the same word with different meanings. I have given here the terms most likely to be encountered by a genealogist investigating the use of computers. Several fuller glossaries are listed in the "Further Reading" section.

8-bit and **16-bit**: see "Bit"

Acoustic coupler: A device which transfers data between a computer and a telephone line. The mouthpiece and earpiece of the telephone are pushed into cups on the coupler. It is an alternative to a modem

Address: The numbered location of a position in the store of a computer. Addresses are used both for locations in immediate access store, and for locations on direct access backing store such as disks.

Algorithm: A definition of a solution to a problem in a finite number of steps.

Analogue Computer: One that holds and manipulates data as continuously variable physical quantities, rather than as discrete digits. (Also spelt Analog).

ASCII (American Standard Code for Information Interchange): The most commonly used code for representing characters on micro-computers.

Assembler: A low level computer language. Generally each statement written by the programmer in assembler is converted to one machine code instruction, whereas a statement in a high level language would be converted to a number of machine code instructions.

Backing Store: Equipment, e.g. magnetic tape and disk, in which a physical medium has to be moved past a reading head to move the stored data into the electronic circuits of the computer.

BASIC: An interactive high level programming language. It is the most widely available language on home computers.

Binary: Numbering system in which any number is represented by combinations of only two different digits, 0 and 1.

Bit: (from BInary digiT) (1) One of the two digits used in the binary system. It is the smallest unit of information. (2) "8-bit", "16-bit", or any other number of bits, as descriptions of computers refer to the number of bits handled at one time by the electronic circuits of the central processor. The number of bits handled in a computation and the number moved about the computer together may be different, so categories are complex. The most significant difference is that an 8-bit computer can only directly address 64 Kbytes of store in one continuous area; 16-bit computers can address much more.

Byte: A group of eight bits treated as a unit. One byte is usually one character.

Cartridge: (1) See "plug-in ROM module". (2) The interchangeable container holding the loop of tape for a Sinclair Microdrive.

Cassette tape: One method of storing data on home computers is to use cassette recorders and tapes manufactured for use in portable sound equipment. Blank cassette tapes can be bought which are packed specially for computer use, in short lengths without non-magnetic leaders.

Central processor: In a micro-computer, the 'processor' chip and the immediate access store. More generally, the part of a computer which controls the other parts and performs operations on data in accordance with the stored program. It includes the part of the computer which performs arithmetic operations and makes logical decisions, the part which controls the flow of data from one place to another, and the immediate access store holding program instructions and data.

Character: One of a set of symbols which can be represented in a computer, e.g. a letter or a digit. It can also mean the space needed in a computer to hold one symbol, normally one byte of eight bits.

Chip: A semiconductor integrated circuit.

Code: (1) The binary digits in a computer which represent a particular character or operation. (2) A computer program, either as held in the computer or as written in statements of a programming language.

Compiler: A program which takes statements in a high level language and converts them into a program in machine code which can be stored away for later use. Once this has been done, the program should run faster than one handled by an interpreter, q.v.

Computer: A machine accepting input, automatically processing it under the control of a stored program and providing the results. A computer includes the means of input, storage, and output (for example a keyboard, disk drive, display and printer) as well as the central processor.

Control key: A key on a computer keyboard which performs a function, rather than generating a character which can be displayed or printed.

CP/M (Control Program for Microcomputers is the most accepted expansion of the abbreviation): A proprietary operating system produced by Digital Research. It is widely used on 8-bit microcomputers, with variants for 16-bit computers, and even for some portable computers without disk storage.

Cursor: A special symbol on a display screen, showing the current typing position.

Daisy wheel printer: One which has its type elements on the flexible spokes of a wheel. To print, the wheel is rotated into position and the character is struck against the ribbon and paper.

Data: Information, held or moved in a coded and structured way, representing numbers, letters, and symbols.

Database: On home computers the term is used for any data handling package. More generally it is a collection of data structured in a way suiting the relationships between elements, independent of particular application programs.

Density: used to express the amount of information recorded per inch, for example on a magnetic tape or along a track on a disk. "Single density" on a 5.25" floppy disk usually implies 2560 bytes around each track, though the term is used with different meanings by different manufacturers. Higher quality diskettes are needed for higher densities of recording.

Digital Computer: One holding and manipulating data as discrete digits.

Direct access: Backing store in which an individual record can be accessed by using its address, for example the track and sector numbers on a disk, rather than by reading a whole file serially until that record is reached.

Directory: A list of the names of files stored on a disk or tape, with their locations, lengths, and sometimes additional information such as the date recorded, password protection, etc.

Disk: A magnetic device storing data on concentric tracks on the surfaces of rotating circular plates (Also spelt **Disc**).

Display: A device on which information is presented visually, e.g. a television screen, other cathode ray tube, or a flat screen on which characters are formed from discrete elements as in a calculator.

DOS (Disk Operating System): The computer programs which control the recording of information on disks.

Dot matrix printer: One in which letters are formed from a pattern of dots. Particularly used for a "Dot matrix impact printer" in which selected members of a row of wires in a printing head are pressed against a ribbon and paper to form characters from dots.

EBCDIC (Extended Binary Coded Decimal Interchange Code): A standard code for representing characters, used mainly on mainframe computers.

Fan fold stationery: A length of paper perforated and folded at regular intervals, with holes along the edge to engage in sprockets or tractors on the printer.

Field: A group of related characters treated as a unit.

File: A group of related records treated as a unit.

Firmware: A program held permanently in read only memory – usually one supplied by the computer manufacturer.

Fixed length field: One in which the space occupied in the store of the computer is not dependent on the information contained in the field, a short piece of information being padded out with spaces to fill the fixed space.

Floating point: Numbers held and manipulated by the central processor in two parts, one representing the digits, the other representing the position of the decimal point in the number. (The first part is the mantissa, the second part is the exponent, and strictly it is the position of the "binary point" not decimal point which is given).

Floppy Disk: A magnetic storage device in which the disk itself is flexible plastic. It is a cheaper device but slower and with less capacity than disks of rigid metal, now called hard disks by contrast.

Flowchart: A diagram using flowlines and standard symbols to show the processing to be performed in a system or program.

Friction feed printer: One in which the paper is pulled through by friction against a drive roller, rather than by sprocket holes.

Genealogy package: A complete pre-written computer program available commercially, designed specifically to store and process genealogical information.

Golf ball (printer or typewriter): One in which the type elements are on the surface of a sphere, rotated to the correct position and struck against the ribbon and paper.

Hard disk: A disk unit in which the recording surface is carried on a rigid metal plate. It is faster and has higher capacity than a floppy disk, q.v.

Hardware: Computer equipment; by contrast, computer programs are "software".

Hexadecimal: Numbers to base 16. By convention digits 0 to 9 and letters A to F represent the numbers from 0 to 15. The contents of 4 bits form one hexadecimal number, so the contents of any byte can be given as two hexadecimal numbers.

High level language: A programming language in which statements are written in terms appropriate to the problem, and translated by a compiler or interpreter into instructions which can be directly obeyed by the computer.

Home computer: A micro–computer with a keyboard and means of display, sold for use in the home.

Immediate access memory: Equipment within a central processor holding data to be available quickly for manipulation.

Ink jet printer: One in which the characters are formed by drops of ink ejected from nozzles onto the paper.

Input: Data transfer from outside the computer system into the central processor via an attached device such as a keyboard.

Instruction: A coded command in a program telling the computer what data to manipulate and what operation to perform on the data.

Integer: A whole number.

Interpreter: A computer program which converts a statement in a high level language into machine code instructions, which are obeyed by the computer before the next statement is interpreted. The machine code is not stored, it is generated afresh each time the statement is used. Most home computers have an interpreter for BASIC held in read only memory.

ISO Code (from the International Standards Organisation) International codes for representing characters in computers. They have provision for national characters such as currency symbols and accented letters, and are very similar to the ASCII code.

Jump: A departure from the normal sequence of processing the instructions in a program. The jump may either be unconditional, or conditional on the result of a test.

Justify: To space out the printing on a line to give even left and right margins.

K (Kilo): K is an abbreviation for Kilo, one thousand. If applied to computer storage one K is a kilobyte and is 1024 bytes (this is convenient to computer designers because 1024 is two to the power of ten).

Load: To move a program or data file from backing store (cassette tape or disk) into the immediate access store of the computer.

Loop: A sequence of instructions which are performed repeatedly until a pre-set condition is reached.

Machine code: A program held in binary digits which can be directly re-cognised and obeyed by the central processor. If the program is stored in this form it will run substantially faster than one written in a high level language such as BASIC and converted by an interpreter as it is run.

Mainframe computer: A large computer providing centralised data processing for an organisation.

Matrix: See "dot matrix".

Medium: Material onto which data is recorded for use in computer peripherals e.g. magnetic tape, floppy disk.

Merge: To combine several sorted files into one, so that the result is in order without further sorting.

Microcomputer: One in which the central processor is a microprocessor

Microdrive: A proprietary term for a device produced by Sinclair Research in which information is recorded on a fast-moving loop of tape in a cartridge, providing random access to data as on a floppy disk.

Microprocessor: A central processor which is all on one semiconductor integrated circuit, except for the immediate access store.

Microsecond: One millionth of a second.

Millisecond: One thousandth of a second.

Minicomputer: A computer, smaller than a mainframe, usually providing a specialised function for an organisation.

Modem (MOdulator DEModulator) A device converting digital computer signals to analogue for transmission on telephone lines.

Monitor: (1) A cathode ray tube display which accepts computer signals directly, contrasted to a television receiver for which computer signals have to be converted to television transmission standards.
(2) A supervisory program, controlling the handling of input and output in a computer.

MSDOS: A proprietary disk operating system produced by Microsoft. It is used on many 16-bit micro-computers. A version of it, PCDOS, is used on IBM personal computers.

Nanosecond: One thousandth of a microsecond.

Near Letter Quality or **NLQ:** Applied to dot matrix printers, it means the letters have closely spaced dots to give improved print quality.

Operating system: Programs controlling the operation of the computer system, particularly the management of files and the sequence of running the programs.

Output: To move the results of processing to a device (such as a display or printer) in a form that can be removed or used.

PCDOS: Operating system for IBM personal computer (see MSDOS also).

Personal computer: A microcomputer intended for use by one person, rather than as a resource shared by many people.

Plug-in ROM module: A program package supplied in the form of a read only memory chip which plugs into a socket in the computer. Sometimes called a "cartridge" if the socket is on the case of the computer rather than on a circuit board.

Program: A structured set of computer instructions which is intended to perform a predetermined task.

Proportional spacing: Printing (like this) in which different letters have different widths, as in hand-writing and printed books. Most typewriters and many computer printers have monospaced type - every letter the same width.

RAM: Random Access Memory

Random Access: Applied to semi-conductor memory, a form of immediate access store such that the program can put data in any location, and subsequently retrieve it. Confusingly the term random access is also used to describe backing store such as disk on which an individual piece of information can be accessed by its address rather than by reading all records before it in the file.

Read only memory: Immediate access store in which data is retained even when the computer is turned off. Data can be read from it but the computer cannot change the data in it.

Record: A related group of fields of data held and moved as one unit.

ROM: See Read Only Memory

RS232: The number of one standard for the signals and interface used in connecting computers over telephone lines.

Sector: On a magnetic disk, the smallest part of a track which can be individually addressed. The capacity of one sector depends on the particular computer: 256 characters would be a typical size.

Sequential access: Used to describe a file organisation in which records are stored and accessed in ascending order of a particular key field such as name, date, or reference number. The term is also used as a synonym for "serial access".

Serial Access: Used to describe backing store such as cassette tape on which a file must be read from the start to reach a particular record, as opposed to direct access.

Side: On a single sided floppy disk, information is recorded on one surface only. On a double sided disk, it is on both surfaces.

Software: Any computer program.

Spreadsheet: A program package which simulates in the computer a sheet of accounting paper, and provides the types of calculation which accountants and business planners perform on rows and columns of figures.

Sprocket: A mechanism on a printer which moves paper by engaging teeth in holes on the side of the paper.

String: A field in which every byte held represents an individual character. It is used particularly for strings of text characters. Other ways of holding data depend on the particular computer and programming language in use. For example, an integer is often held as two consecutive bytes taken together, a floating point number might be held as four consecutive bytes taken together.

Tear down paper: Fan fold stationery perforated along the sides so that the strip with the sprocket holes can be torn off.

Thimble: A printing element, like a daisy wheel but thimble shaped.

Track: On a disk, one of a set of concentric circular areas on which information is recorded.

Tractor: A sprocket mechanism on a printer, in particular one in which the sprockets are not carried on the platen spindle.

Variable length field: One in which the storage space occupied by the field is adjusted to the length of the information contained within it, by contrast with a fixed length field.

Word processor: A system for keying the text of a document into the store of a computer. Corrections can be made by addition, deletion, insertion, searching and moving of letters, words and paragraphs. Also used for formatting of printed text.

Write protect: On a floppy disk, an adhesive tab can be stuck over a square sided notch in the cardboard cover to tell the computer not to change the data recorded on that disk.

Wysiwyg (What you see is what you get): A word processing package in which the screen display is in the format in which the information will be printed on paper.

Note: A letter G indicates an entry in the Glossary.
The Appendices are not indexed.